Winter Edition

The New Women of Color Daily Devotional Winter 2nd Edition

The articles and prayers are taken from the Women of Color Devotional Bible © World Bible/Nia Publishing Co.

Urban Spirit! Publishing and Media Company is an African American owned company based in Atlanta, GA. You can find more information at http://www.urbanspirit.biz/

The New Women of Color Daily Devotional Winter Edition © Urban Spirit! Publishing and Media Company

Produced with the assistance of Cheryl Wilson, i4Details and Ashley Taylor and Larry Taylor, Livingstone, LLC.

Photos: iStock/Getty images
All rights reserved. No portion of this publication may be reproduced, stored in a retrieval system, or transmitted in any form by any means—electronic, mechanical, photocopy, recording, or otherwise—without the prior written permission of the publisher, except for brief quotations in critical reviews or articles.

All Scripture quotes, unless otherwise indicated, are from the Authorized King James Version of the Bible.

Scripture quotes marked amplified are from the Amplified Bible, © Copyright 1954, 1958, 1962, 1964, 1965, 1987 by The Lockman Foundation.

Scripture quotes marked NIV are taken from the HOLY BIBLE, NEW INTERNATIONAL VERSION®. Copyright© 1973, 1978, 1984 by the International Bible Society.

Scripture quotes marked NLT are taken from the Holy Bible, New Living Translation, copyright © 1996. Used by permission of Tyndale House Publishers, Inc, Wheaton, Illinois 60189. All rights reserved.

ISBN: 978-1-958779-00-2: Urban Spirit

ISBN: 978-1-958779-02-6: Choice Books

Manufactured in the United States of America

www.urbanspirit.biz

DECEMBER - JANUARY - FEBRUARY

Special thanks to:
Stephanie Perry Moore, *General Editor*
Charrita Danley Quimby, *Content Editor*
Brionna S. Jones, *Editorial Assistant*

TABLE OF CONTENTS

Month	Week	Theme	Contributor	Page
December	1	Warmth	Tia McCollors	8
December	2	Comfort	Sherryll Atkins	28
December	3	Hibernate	Rev. Mariah Crews	48
December	4	Decorate	Rev. Dr. Robin E. Henderson-Wilson	68
December	5	Celebration	Rev. Dr. Billie Boyd-Cox	88
January	6	Wonder	Kayla A. Monroe	108
January	7	Fire	Evangelist Terri L. Hannett	133
January	8	Light	First Lady Kelli Jones	152
January	9	Go	Minister Shantel M. Moore	172
February	10	Listen	C. Denise Hendricks	188
February	11	Increase	First Lady Jamell Meeks	209
February	12	Learn	Dr. Laquanda Carpenter	228
February	13	Lead	Karen Lascaris	248

Contributors' bios may be found following the devos.

Dear Precious Woman of Color,

Winter is a miraculous time to celebrate with God and appreciate the reason for the season. How can that happen? Well, while the air is cool and crisp, curl up with this book and get closer to God. The same way Mary gave birth to our Savior, you can walk into the New Year giving birth to your dreams. Thirteen superb women from across the country have etched devotionals (devos) that speak to significant topics for wintertime.

The sole purpose of this book is to offer encouragement to you. The design of the book allows you to choose five days every week and dig into the devos. The goal is that they will warm your soul and help you live even better for God. Each devo has a title, a thought-provoking question, a scripture, a short story, an application, and a closing prayer. When positioned together into a daily devotional, the blend is a guiding tool to help you go deeper into the Word.

It is our desire that the words on each page speak directly to your spirit. May your journey during the months of December through February bring **WARMTH** to your life. May it bring **COMFORT** in the tough times and help you **HIBERNATE** when you simply need a break. May this help you **DECORATE** your space with glee and have a lovely Christmas **CELBRATION**. May it help you to know that He is a **WONDER** that gives **FIRE** in the cold and **LIGHT** in the darkness. May this book also help you **GO** and live for Him, while you **LISTEN** to what He is calling you to do in the New Year. Lastly, I pray you love and **LIKE** yourself, **LEARN** to be satisfied and follow the One who wants to **LEAD** you to your destiny!

God bless,

Stephanie Perry Moore
General Editor

WARMTH - TIA MCCOLLORS

DECEMBER
WEEK 1

DAY 1
RECEIVING WARMTH FROM YOUR FRIENDS

Do you have friendships that warm your soul?

"Ointment and perfume rejoice the heart: so doth the sweetness of a man's friend by hearty counsel."
(PROVERBS 27:9)

STORY

Krystal knew her announcement at the weekly meeting would be met with eye rolls and sighs. There was no way to avoid staying late to pull the necessary reports and she hated to have to tell her team, especially on a Friday afternoon. Since Krystal's promotion, some of the colleagues she used to go out to lunch with seemed to avoid her. She was thankful for the salary increase because she definitely needed it. Her hard work and commitment had opened the door for the promotion opportunity; no one could deny that. However, her higher aspirations led to fewer friends.

"Hey there, girl," Lisa said, walking in with two steaming mugs of coffee. She put one of them down in front of Krystal then took the seat across from her desk. "We're going to need it," she sighed.

Krystal was relieved to see her friend's face. They had been colleagues for the last six years and Lisa had been more excited for Krystal's promotion than anyone. They had even met early every morning to pray about it the week leading up to the round of interviews.

"You're doing a great job," Lisa continued. "Don't worry about Joe's snide remarks. It has nothing to do with you and everything to do with him. God is by your side and I am too."

APPLICATION

Often times, the things we pray for become the circumstances that lead us to challenges. Those challenges are not only opportunities for personal growth, but they also serve as reasons for us to lean into God. One of the ways God blesses our lives is to surround us with supportive friends. His Word teaches us that great friendships refresh our soul. We're born for adversity and friendships make us wiser.

RECEIVING WARMTH FROM YOUR FRIENDS

What kind of friend are you? Often times we're prevented from spending quality time with friends because of our busy lifestyles, over scheduled calendars, or our daily responsibilities of work and family. However, small acts carry heavy weight. A simple text of encouragement, a surprise meal delivery, or calling to pray with your friend are expressions of love.

There is a saying, "Good friends are like quilts. They age with you and never lose their warmth."

PRAYER

Dear Lord, place me around friends that intend the best for me. Surround me with a circle of friends who cheer on my triumphs, encourage me during disappointments, and pray for Your will in my life. Even more so, allow me to be a strong friend. Let me be the kind of friend that gives good and wise counsel. If I have offended my friends in any way, show me how to repair those offenses. Restore the broken friendships in my life that were affected by misunderstandings. Even for those friendships that may not be meant for me, let our words toward each other be seasoned with grace. Lord, I want to honor the friendships that You have given me. Let us carry one another's burdens and be righteous in our dealings with each other. In Jesus' name, I pray, Amen.

DAY 2
GIVING WARMTH TO YOUR FAMILY

Do you give your family a warm place to live?

"Behold, how good and how pleasant it is for brethren to dwell together in unity!"
(PSALM 133:1)

STORY

"Does anyone in this house care that we are living in a pig pen besides me?" Krystal fussed. She stepped over the abandoned board game in the middle of the living room floor. Her son hadn't even bothered to load the dishwasher and she didn't even want to think about the

countless loads of dirty laundry upstairs. Krystal was tired, frustrated, and hungry. She had never intended to spend her Saturday morning finishing reports.

Her husband, Bernard, walked in from the garage with two pizza boxes. "Dinner is served and movie night is up," he exclaimed.

"I don't have time for movie night. I have too much work to do," Krystal replied.

Bernard slid her laptop from her grasp and put it out of reach behind his back. "You need a break. And *we* need *you*," he sharply stated.

Krystal's sons were already snuggled into their favorite spots on the couch. How was it that just yesterday they were six and eight years old and now they were twelve and fourteen years old? It was a miracle in itself that they were both in one room and not closed behind bedroom doors, shutting out the entire world with headphones and technology.

"Only if you bring me my fuzzy socks and a warm blanket," Krystal remarked. She squeezed between the boys on the couch and kissed them on the cheek. They didn't protest like usual. In that moment, she didn't care about dirty dishes or dirty clothes. She would savor the moment of being together with her family.

APPLICATION

It is okay to slow down and do nothing. Society has conditioned us to believe that if we aren't working on a project, looking for the next big thing or being productive in other ways that we are wasting our lives. Rest, however, is also a part of having a productive life. Resting allows us to relax, recharge, and refocus. Not only do we benefit from moments of downtime, but our families do as well.

Our family circle benefits from a wife, mother, sister, or aunt who has made it a priority to spend time with God. In our devotion to Him, we are shown how to care for our families, speak words of wisdom and discern their needs. Remember to smile when your children enter the room and be attentive to your husband when he arrives home from work. Not only will it make them feel good, it will make you feel good, too.

PRAYER

Dear God, allow me to see my family in the way that You see them. Let me see their hurts as clearly as I see their accomplishments. Help me to be patient with them. Help me to speak to them in love and with understanding. My desire is to raise a family in the admonition of the Lord. Order my steps and light my path on this journey. I am not perfect, but I am willing. Lord, let my home be a safe space my family and I can be transparent. Let it be a place where I come for healing. Let it be the place where I am corrected without being judged. If my home is the training ground for how I operate in the world, then let my family be a godly example of how to act justly, love mercifully and walk humbly with You. In Jesus' name, I pray, Amen.

DAY 3
SHOWING WARMTH IN YOUR SERVICE

Have you warmed someone's heart through service?

"Look not every man on his own things, but every man also on the things of others."
(PHILIPPIANS 2:4)

STORY

Terrence pulled a sweatshirt from his father's alma mater over his head. "Mom, I'm going to the gym with Jalen. We're going to shoot some hoops. Basketball tryouts are coming up," Terrence informed his mother.

Krystal zipped up her jacket and put on her hat and gloves. She wasn't sure if her assigned post would be outside or inside, but she would be ready. At church last Sunday, she had signed her family up to volunteer at one of the warming stations around town. As meteorologists had predicted, the temperatures would dip below freezing that night and probably the rest of the week.

"You can go, but it has to be after we finish," Krystal said.

Terrence shrugged and tossed the basketball in the back of the trunk.

Krystal and Bernard handed out new socks, blankets, and gloves to those arriving at the warming station. The things that she took for granted were the necessities that others waited in line to receive. Krystal's accomplishments at work were one thing, but having her family be of service to the community was even more of an accomplishment. Raising her sons to have a sense of service and be a value to the community had always been important to her and Bernard.

Terrence approached Krystal. "Hey, Mom. One of the little kids over there said he likes basketball. Do you mind if I get my ball and bounce it around outside with him?"

Krystal smiled and replied, "Of course you can."

People may have come out of the blistering cold to warm their bodies, but her son's thoughtfulness today had also warmed his mother's heart.

APPLICATION

One of the most important jobs we have is to be the hands and feet of Jesus. The Bible reminds us that we should treat others good, if it is in our power to do so. Open your eyes and your heart to the needs of others. When we carry the burdens of others, we fulfill the law of Christ.

Jesus lived a life serving others. His healing ministry gave sight to the blind and strength to a lame man's legs. He met a need. Jesus multiplied five loaves of bread and two fish so that He would be able to feed thousands. He met a need. Even when Jesus performed His first miracle at the wedding and turned water into wine, He was meeting a need. No task was beneath Him. Jesus even washed His disciples' feet!

Throughout the Bible, Jesus admonishes us to follow His example. In what ways can you use your life to meet the needs of others? How does the way you serve others shine a light on God's unconditional love?

PRAYER

Dear God, teach me Your ways. Show me how to serve as You would serve. I quiet my life and my schedule so that I can see the needs of other people daily. Turn my heart toward those who need my help. Show me how to use the gifts You have given me to lift up others. I haven't always done what I could do and should do. I've been selfish in times that I should've been selfless. I repent, in the name of Jesus. Please turn my heart toward the things that matter most to You. I don't come to be served, but to serve. Show me the beauty of servanthood. In Jesus' name, I pray, Amen.

www.urbanspirit.biz

DAY 4
SPREADING WARMTH IN THE WORKPLACE

Does your warmth in the workplace build a good reputation?

"Heaviness in the heart of man maketh it stoop: but a good word maketh it glad."
(PROVERBS 12:25)

STORY

Over the last two months the conference room had been reserved for department meetings and as extra working space for the auditors. When she called her team to an emergency lunch

meeting, Krystal heard the grumbling through her closed office door. Little did they know what awaited them. The murmuring and complaining turned to cheers when they walked into a fully catered lunch from one of the nearby popular lunch spots.

Krystal pushed past everyone until she was at the front of the room and stated, "I wanted to show my appreciation for all of your sacrifices. You all have families, hobbies, and other commitments that you've had to balance. It's difficult juggling all of those commitments, but you've managed to pull it off." Krystal was surprised when she heard Joe yell from the back.

"We love you, Krystal!" Joe shouted.

Lisa gave her a wink. Maybe Joe didn't hate her after all. The lunch was a small demonstration of her appreciation, but it was important that she validated their feelings. Her mind began racing, thinking of ways she could honor their work and implement an "open door" policy for better communication with her colleagues. This was an important part of the job, too.

APPLICATION

God orders our steps, and that includes where He places us in the workplace. Whether our reason for the job is to gain more experience in order to find better employment, or climb the ladder of success at the same corporation, we should look for ways to make it an enjoyable experience for ourselves and others. Even with an inconsiderate boss, stay clear of work place gossip. It's possible to offer a listening ear without participating in malicious talk.

The Bible tells us to work with all of our hearts and to do it unto the Lord. Word travels fast within a company and that includes good words. When you build a reputation for being kind, trustworthy, and committed, you set yourself apart from others. Doors of opportunities do not open only by the work of your hands, but also the work of your heart.

PRAYER

God, I bless and thank You for the job You have given me. You are ultimately my provider. My job is a gift from You that allows me to take care of my family, myself, and even invest in my hopes and dreams. When there are times that I have to sacrifice my time with my family for my job responsibilities, restore the time in other ways. There are times when my job has called me to murmur and complain. I won't jump on the bandwagon of dissenters. I'll bridle my tongue and speak life. I'll find joy in my job and help others to do the same. When it's in my power to do so, I'll acknowledge the sacrifice of others both publicly and privately and ensure they are justly compensated. Help me to do my work unto You and not unto man. In Jesus' name, I pray, Amen.

www.urbanspirit.biz

DAY 5
RECEIVING WARMTH FROM THE FATHER

Have you hidden yourself under the warmth of God's wings?

"He shall cover thee with his feathers, and under his wings shalt thou trust: his truth shall be thy shield and buckler."
(PSALM 91:4)

STORY

Krystal crawled into bed and pulled the comforter up to her waist. The day had been exhausting, yet fulfilling, and she needed to end it in the same way it began—with prayer and devotion to the Lord. Usually, Krystal began her nighttime Bible reading with Psalm 91. It had been a habit ever since her grandmother led her to the scripture one lonely night when she was away at college. After so many years later, Krystal had committed the entire chapter to memory.

No matter the circumstance, God was always by Krystal's side. Whether her job felt rewarding or crushing, He was there. Whether her sons showed their gratitude or their agitation, He was there. God had threaded the strands of her life in such a way that it was a beautiful tapestry of experiences. Only He had worked all the things in her life, both good and bad, out for her good.

Bernard walked in and held up his hand. "More fuzzy socks," he said, lifting the covers and sliding them onto her feet. They were warm, but nothing like the warmth she felt from God's protection.

APPLICATION

There is no greater joy than knowing that God cares for you. Nothing you can do can separate you from the love of God. His love extends beyond any other love you've ever known.

How do you draw closer to God? Begin by spending more time in His Word. As you mediate on God's Word, you will come to know His character and heart. Likewise, when you spend time in prayer, both talking and listening to Him, you will be able to discern His still small voice.

Always know that God wants the best for you. His plan for your life is more than you can imagine. Can you believe that? What He has for you is bigger than your wildest dreams! Solely depend on the Lord and trust Him in the process. Begin to write out your dreams and prayers in a Bible so you can look back and remember the way He has orchestrated your life. A written account of His faithfulness will also grow the faith of your family for years to come. Let them see God through you.

PRAYER

Lord, I thank You for the future and the hope that You have planned for me. I'm amazed at Your grace. I'm amazed at Your love. You will never leave me nor forsake me and I'm grateful for that. I want to know You better each and every day. I will cherish the time that we spend together because our relationship is important to me. Heavenly Father, You know what's best for me. I will continue to put my hope and trust in You. In Jesus' name, I pray, Amen.

COMFORT – SHERRYLL ATKINS

DECEMBER
WEEK 2

DAY 1
COMFORT IN DEATH

Has a loved one died?

"Then cometh the end, when he shall have delivered up the kingdom to God, even the Father; when he shall have put down all rule and all authority and power."

(I CORINTHIANS 15:24)

STORY

Glorya's father lay peacefully on the hospital bed as if nothing had happened, as if he had not just…died. This was the man who had once held eight-year-old Glorya on his shoulders so she could see Michael do the robot at her first Jackson 5 concert. He had also been the

one who comforted Glorya during the worst days of her ugly-duckling adolescent stage.

"You are as pretty as a speckled pup," her dad had declared, using a cherished southern simile.

"Really, Daddy?" Glorya asked, unconvinced.

Her dad nodded. "If I'm lying, I'm flying."

As much as she loved her mom, it was her dad's affirmations that got Glorya through her teen years. When his deep voice reassured her, she believed him.

Glorya recalled being a sophomore in college and her father driving all the way from the San Francisco Bay Area to Los Angeles just to change the oil in her car. Then he took her to dinner. He was the best dad in the world.

"What would you like us to do with the body?" the nurse asked, breaking into Glorya's reverie.

"The body?" Glorya mumbled. How could the man who had raised, taught, and protected her become "the body?" It was all so surreal. How could her beloved daddy be dead?

APPLICATION

Death in any form is a shock to our system. In the story of creation, there was no mention of death because God is life and that which He made was made to live forever in Him. Death is a consequence of sin, beginning with Adam and Eve. Every time something or someone dies, our spirits are reminded of

COMFORT IN DEATH

what we had, what we were, and what we lost. This is the true reason death makes us sad and produces such profound grief.

Dying is *not* a natural part of life as is often quoted. It is wholly unnatural. Our souls yearn for immortality because it is a return to God's original intent of perfection for us. The road back to perfection starts with believing in the birth, death, and resurrection of the Father's only begotten Son, Jesus Christ. Without Him, we are forced to mourn like the heathen who has no hope, which results in despair. With Him, we know to be absent from the body is to be present with the Lord.

The passing of loved ones compounds our heartache. When you encounter death, let the Holy Spirit be your shock absorber and comforter. He collects every one of your tears in a bottle and keeps them in a book of remembrance. He has promised to be near and heal the brokenhearted. His compassion is infinite. God hears all prayers, whether they are spoken, sighed, or cried. He will hear you.

PRAYER

Dear God, I am trying to process the idea of death and the reality of separation from someone so dear to my heart that it feels as though my whole world has collapsed with their departure. Outside, the world goes on as usual. The sky is still overhead. People are driving, going to work, laughing, joking, and living while I am now forced to refer to my loved one in the past tense. I don't even know what to think. I feel like I'm frozen in time—or maybe I'm numb. I'm not sure. What I do know is that I need You in a real way right now. Not Sunday service real—I mean, for *real* real. I am depending on Your grace to see me through. In Jesus' name, I pray, Amen.

www.urbanspirit.biz

DAY 2
COMFORT IN MOURNING

Is there good grief?

"Blessed are they that mourn: for they shall be comforted."
(MATTHEW 5:4)

STORY

Glorya sat opposite Mr. Edwards, the funeral director. She waited while Mr. Edwards finished typing in the last of the information necessary to order the death certificate for her father.

He turned to Glorya. "It's almost three years to the day since we were here doing this for your mother," Mr. Edwards said. "Your father sat in that exact chair, right next to you."

Glorya did not turn to look at the empty chair. She nodded. "Yes. I want to thank you for your kindness and competence in handling the arrangements, Mr. Edwards." Glorya paused. "For both of my parents," she added.

Mr. Edwards continued, "I did not have the pleasure of meeting your mother, but I really liked your dad." He paused. "You seem remarkably composed, considering. How are you *really* doing?"

Glorya responded, her voice steady and somewhat detached. "I have a lot to do, Mr. Edwards—probate, sell the house. There is no time for tears."

Mr. Edwards said gently, "Grief has its own timetable. Though it tarries, it won't be late."

Mr. Edwards returned to his paperwork, leaving Glorya to ponder his words.

APPLICATION

There is much to be done after someone dies, including determining the process for the disposal of the remains, processing death certificates and planning services. Perhaps property must be sold, pension payments stopped, or inheritances distributed. The list goes on and on.

All of this post-death activity allows us to disregard the fact that someone we love has died, departed this life, transitioned, etc. Whatever euphemism we choose, the reality is that holidays and birthdays will never ever be the same. This can be side-stepped while we confer with the caterer about the repast. Immediately following the loss, the knowledge that we can no longer call or visit our loved one is deferred as we bury ourselves in the busyness of trusts, wills, and probate.

The Bible tells us that blessed are they who mourn for they shall be comforted. Before we can be comforted, mourning is indeed required. Regardless of the loss—a loved one, a relationship, a job, or a pet—it is necessary to express our sorrow, lest we be stuck in an emotional constipation that disallows our ability to truly move forward.

The God of unfathomable compassion knows and understands our pain. The Bible reminds us that He heals the broken in heart and binds up their wounds. Those who grieve are wounded. Treat your grief with consistent doses of the Word of God as well as healthy emotional expression. You will get through this season. You really will.

PRAYER

Lord, I have so much to do that I do not have time to mourn. Maybe I'm also using my busyness as a way to stave off releasing what feels like a geyser of grief. I cannot stand to think about what life will be like without my loved one. To be honest, I'm afraid that if I start crying, I will never stop. You said in Your Word that when my father and my mother forsake me, then the Lord will take me up. I feel abandoned. Take me up, Lord, as You promised. You told me not to fear because You will never leave me nor forsake me. In Jesus' name, I pray, Amen.

DAY 3
COMFORT OF ACCEPTANCE

Does joy come when you're mourning?

"For I have satisfied the weary soul, and I have replenished every sorrowful soul."
(JEREMIAH 31:25)

STORY

It had taken Glorya five months to empty her parents' house. She was astonished to find a clay handprint of her own five-year-old hand carefully packed away in her mother's closet, along with a host of other mementoes. Glorya put her hand over the clay keepsake. Her adult fingers scarcely eclipsed the small imprint.

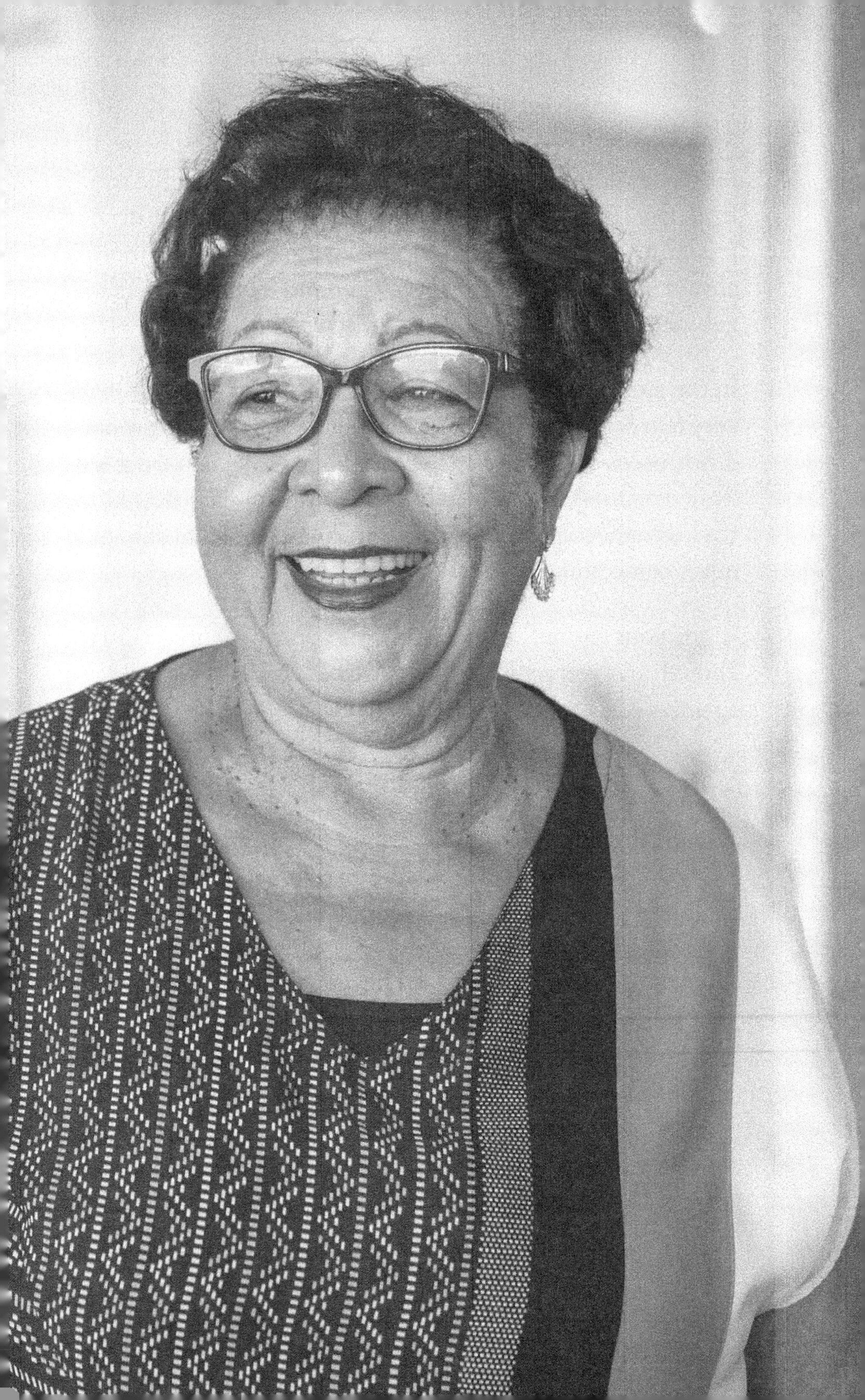

Standing in the barren family room, Glorya remembered her father patiently issuing instructions as she slowly pulled away from the curb in his prized bronze Audi for her first driving lesson. She felt the warmth of the kitchen where her mother always had something to eat for her and her friends, as well as extended family and whoever else visited.

In the sterile silence of the empty house, Glorya felt as if the very marrow of her bones was soaked in sorrow. She dropped down on the floor where her mother's easy chair once sat, leaned against the wall, and wept. Pent up tears flowed for the loss of her beloved parents. It hurt knowing that she could never come home to see them again.

"I am your home," the voice of the Spirit assured Glorya. Though her weeping subsided, Glorya knew she would cry again.

APPLICATION

To mourn someone who was dear to you, is to recognize that you had the good fortune to love someone. To love is to exhibit the very essence of God, for God is love. God not only understands grief, but He has a vivid and intimate experience with it. He sent Jesus to die on the cross for our sins.

To cry, weep and wail is part of the process of letting go of our dear loved ones who have departed this life. It has been noted that those who express their sorrow at the outset are the most expeditious at working through the grieving process. There is something very cleansing about crying. Tears carry the very essence of sorrow out of our insides; therefore, there is no tear wasted. God collects our tears and even keeps them in His book. You do not mourn alone. Your sorrow is precious to God.

PRAYER

Lord, my eyes are red and swollen. My heart is broken in fragments and shards. My soul is weighted with the boulder of bereavement. All my life I have heard the elders say, "Hold on to God's unchanging hand." But, in Your Word You said that You do not change. My whole world has changed. I need You, God, to hold my hand. The Bible reminds me that You are near to those who have a broken heart. Help me to feel the nearness of You, Oh Lord. Comfort me, Oh Lord. In Jesus' name, I pray, Amen.

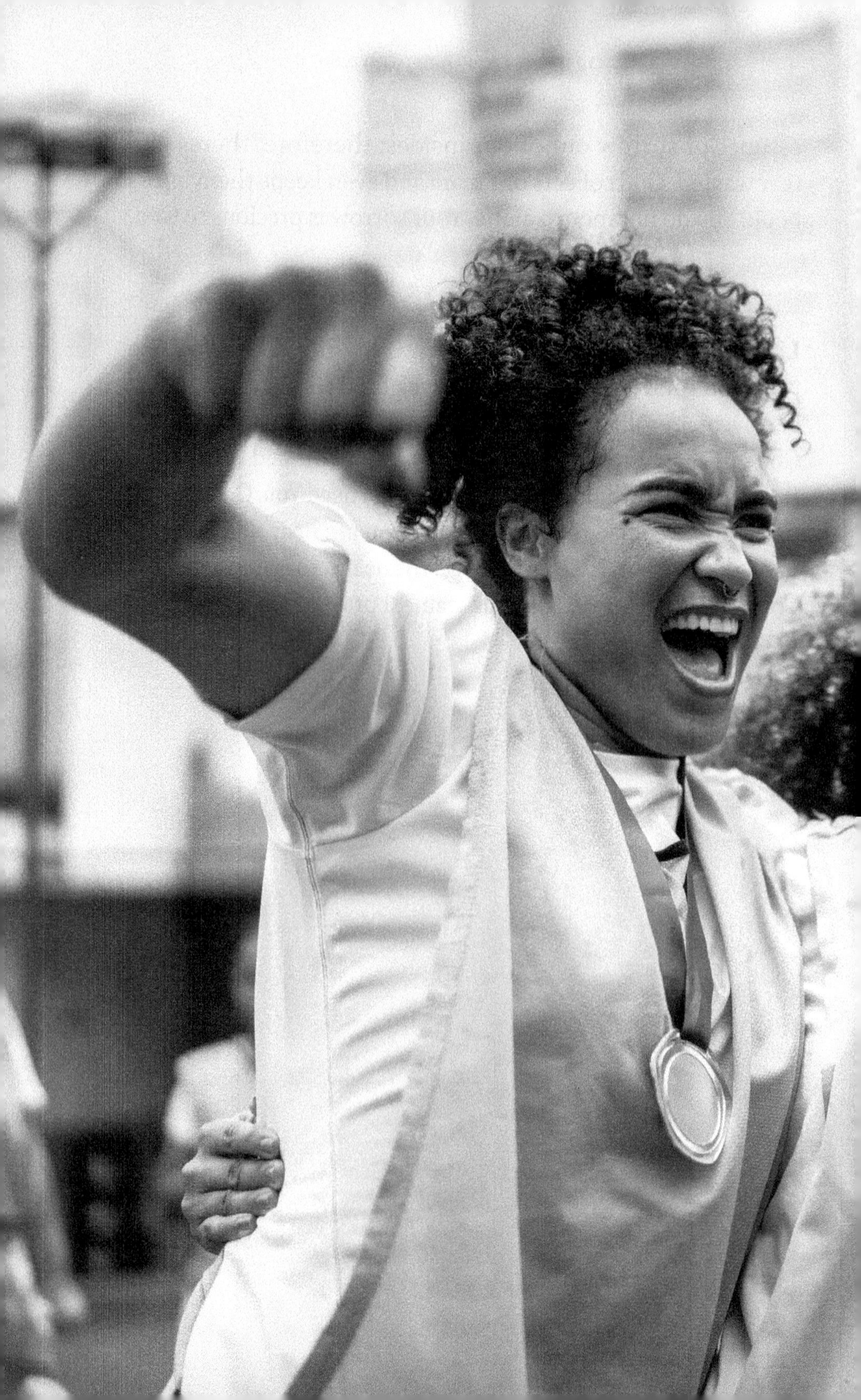

DAY 4
COMFORT OF LAUGHTER

Is there humor in heartache?

"Blessed be God, even the Father of our Lord Jesus Christ, the Father of mercies, and the God of all comfort; Who comforteth us in all our tribulation, that we may be able to comfort them which are in any trouble, by the comfort wherewith we ourselves are comforted of God."
(II CORINTHIANS 1:3-4)

STORY

"Hello, Tina? It's Glorya."

"Glorya? Oh my goodness. Girl, how long has it been?"

Glorya laughed. "It's been a minute."

"More like a decade," Tina chuckled.

"I know, right? I saw on Facebook that your father passed. DM'ing condolences is so impersonal. I wanted to call, see how you're doing."

Tina's cheerful veneer fell away. She said quietly, "Thank you. It's been hard. I can barely sleep. I have far too many memories."

Glorya's heart went out to her friend. In an effort to give Tina a brief moratorium to her mourning, Glorya asked, "Speaking of memories, do you remember taking shop class?"

Tina burst out laughing. "I learned how to loosen a lug nut, change a tire, and dang near how to assemble an entire car from scratch, just to be close to Octavius Butcher."

Glorya and Tina spontaneously broke into the Commodores song, "Just to be clooooose to youuuu, giirrrl..."

By the time Glorya and Tina hung up two hours later, Tina was crying from laughing so hard. Glorya was surprised at how much better she felt, too.

APPLICATION

We've heard it before. Helping your fellow man is the best way to help yourself. It looks great on paper, but when getting out of bed takes all of the energy you have, the last thing on your mind is considering how you can be of service to someone else. The Bible tells us to think on the things that are good, pure, perfect, lovely, honest, just, and of good report. If anything has any virtue or any praise, we are commanded to think on these things. For that effort, we are promised that God's peace that surpasses all understanding shall mount guard over our hearts and minds.

Here's the cheat sheet. Think about God. The more you think about Him, the more He is magnified. A magnifying glass makes the thing you're looking at seem so much bigger than surrounding objects, even if those objects are physically larger. Every time you count your blessings, one-by-one, you are making God greater than anything you face or even feel. Name each blessing slowly. Take a deep, cleansing breath. Name another blessing. Take another breath. Bless and breathe. Breathe and bless.

You never know what showing the smallest act of kindness can do because you don't know what a person is going through. Smile at a stranger; hold open a door; call a friend and encourage them. It is amazing how much better you feel when you make the effort to brighten someone's day.

PRAYER

God, it's hard to think about helping other people when I am so engulfed in a sea of sadness. Please help me to magnify You by counting my blessings, one-by-one. I pray for all of the people across the earth who are going through this process. I no longer sympathize with those that mourn. I greatly empathize. Therefore, my prayer has now become the effectual fervent prayer. Please cover us with Your compassion as we cry out to You. Introduce Yourself to the lost that they may take part in Your mercy and Your grace while they lament. Thank You, Lord, for helping me to think about and pray for others, many of whom do not know how to call on You. In Jesus' name, I pray, Amen.

www.urbanspirit.biz

DAY 5
COMFORT OF PROMISE

Is there life after breath?

*"Thou hast turned for me my mourning into dancing:
thou hast put off my sackcloth,
and girded me with gladness."*
(PSALM 30:11)

STORY

Following her chat with Tina, Glorya decided to have a collective celebration of life for her friends and their friends who had lost loved ones. Glorya wanted to offer a space to anyone who needed comfort, conversation, and company. Glorya invited her pastor to say a few words.

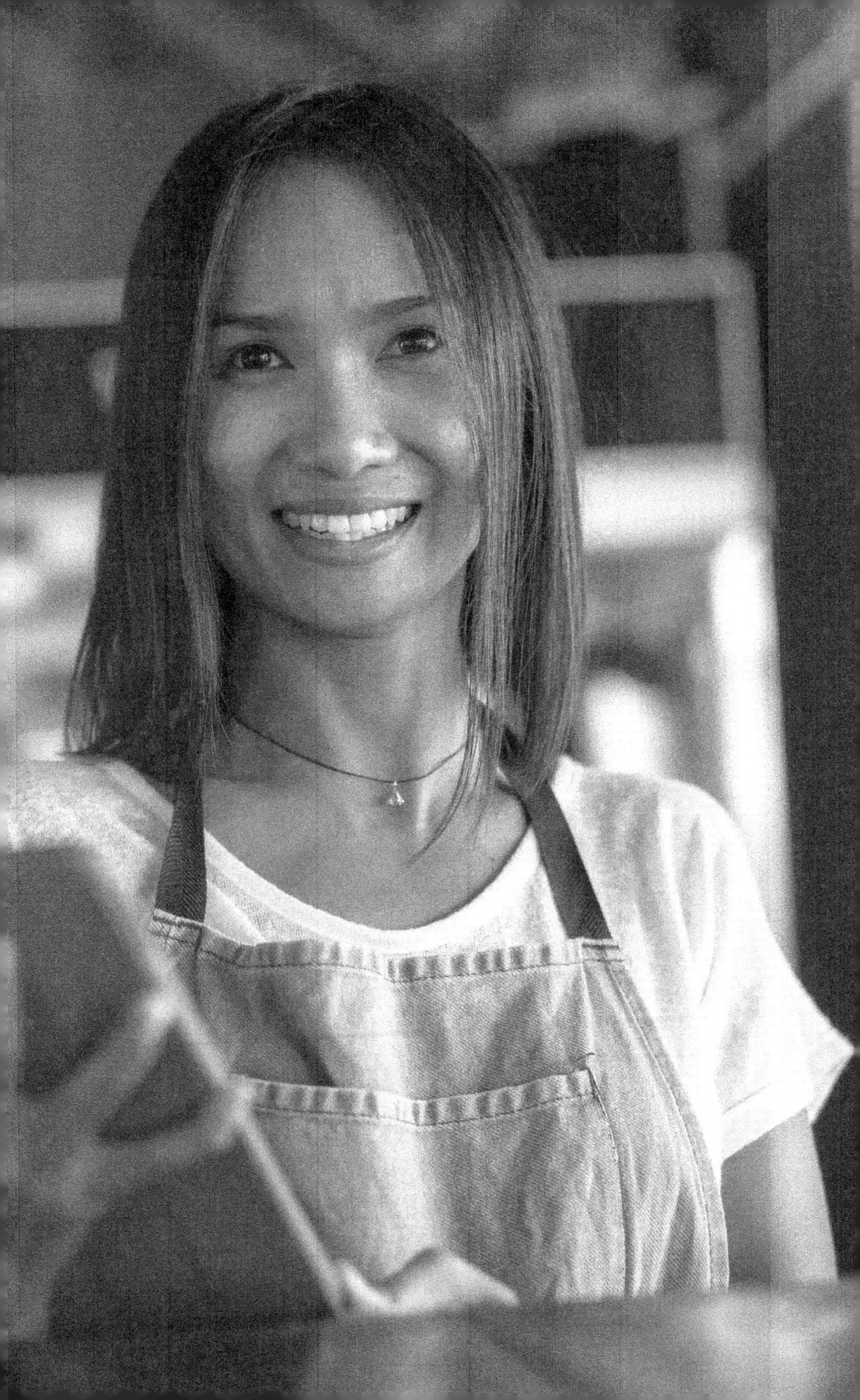

In his remarks, her pastor talked about the various stages of grief. He reminded everyone that it is a process. "You will not get over the loss immediately," he said. "You must allow yourself to express your emotions. Take everything to God in prayer. He will comfort you and help you through the process."

Everyone present was given an opportunity to say a few words about their loss. Their comments were uplifting and encouraging. Overall, the response to CCL was so positive that Glorya was bombarded with emails and phone calls about hosting another one.

APPLICATION

The display of grief often triggers a subconscious fear of the debt we all must pay, death. The wages of sin are unavoidable; however, what can be avoided is Hell. The Bible is very clear about how to be saved. You must believe in your heart that God raised Jesus from the dead.

As the Bible states it is not His will that any should perish, but that all should come to repentance. You cannot die in Christ for He is The Way, The Truth, and The Life! Hallelujah! If you believe and accept Christ as your Savior, you will have eternal life.

PRAYER

Lord, You said in Your Word that when the perishable has been clothed with the imperishable and the mortal with immortality, then death is swallowed up in victory. This is a promise made by

Your saints that causes us to ask with joy, "Oh death, where is thy sting?" I pray for those who do not know You and are hopeless, tormented by the fear of what happens after we die. Call them out of darkness and into Your marvelous light, Lord, the same as You did for me. Your will be done in all things. In Jesus' name, I pray, Amen.

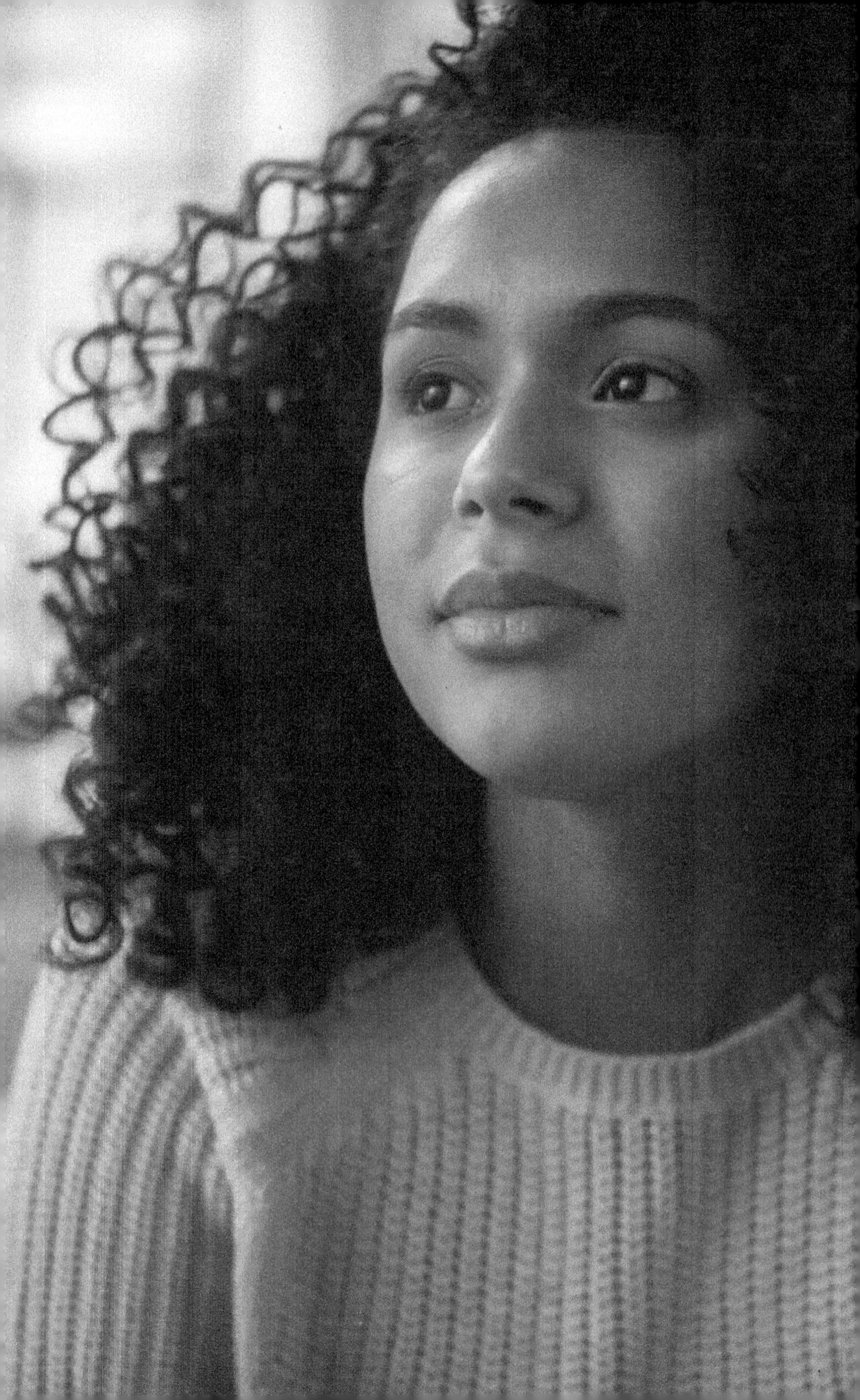

HIBERNATE – REV. MARIAH CREWS

DECEMBER
WEEK 3

DAY 1
EMBRACE YOUR HIBERNATION

Why do we resist hibernation?

"I beseech you therefore, brethren, by the mercies of God, that ye present your bodies a living sacrifice, holy, acceptable unto God, which is your reasonable service. And be not conformed to this world: but be ye transformed by the renewing of your mind, that ye may prove what is that good, and acceptable, and perfect, will of God."

(ROMANS 12:1-2)

STORY

Tiana spent her entire life searching for something. Something different, something new, something...better.

As a recent college graduate, she was surrounded by people who knew (or at least pretended to know) exactly who they were. Why didn't she? Why didn't she know what she wanted to do, or whom she was supposed to be?

"It has been months!" Tiana said to her mother in exasperation. "Why haven't I heard from God yet, Momma? I am doing everything right. I'm on my knees each morning, but I still haven't heard anything."

Tiana's mom smiled and said, "Baby girl, when you pray, are you praying out of practice or purpose? When you are seeking an answer from God, you can't pray the way you always pray. You have to pray with *intention*."

So, the next morning, when Tiana woke up and knelt down to pray, she prayed with *intention*. She asked God to show her how to grow from who she was into whom she was called and created to be. She was specific in her prayer. Afterward, she finally heard God speak. She heard Him say that she could not see her path clearly because her vision had become blurred by the world and her past. God told her that in order for her to see what He had in store for her future, she needed to withdraw. She needed to hibernate.

APPLICATION

The idea of transformation is one of true beauty. So many of us are seeking transformation in one way or another. When the Bible encourages us to transform, it tells us about the sacrifice that true transformation requires. In order not to conform to the patterns of this world, you have to distance yourself from the world first. You have to hibernate, and that is scary.

The realization that we need to hibernate can be really intimidating. The idea that we have to close ourselves off from the world, from certain relationships, or even our own habits is terrifying. However, if you are seeking the type of transformation that breaks generational curses, heals decades of hurt and pain, or sets you free from whatever holds the enemy has on you, then you have to embrace the period of hibernation that is necessary for that transformation to take place.

Take some time to write what frightens you as it relates to your hibernation season. Are you worried that you will miss out on something? Are you worried about whom you will become on the other side of this season? Are you worried about the sacrifice that is required? Write everything down, so that you can be specific in your prayers and God can provide you with peace and replace the anxiety that you feel. Remember, pray with intention.

PRAYER

Mighty God, wonderful counselor, and everlasting friend, thank You for the gift of hibernation. Thank You for the reminder that I am still growing and transforming into whom You have created me to be. Thank You for not allowing me to get comfortable in complacency and for calling me to do more, be better, and strive for greater. I pray that when I begin to get overwhelmed by what this hibernation will require of me—or will change in me—that You might meet me in the midst of my anxiety. I pray that You will comfort me, encourage me, and help me rest in the knowledge that You will be with me even in the midst of my hibernation. In the name of Jesus, I pray, Amen.

DAY 2
PREPARE FOR HIBERNATION

What are you taking with you, and what are you leaving behind?

"That ye put off concerning the former conversation the old man, which is corrupt according to the deceitful lusts; And be renewed in the spirit of your mind."

(EPHESIANS 4:22-23)

STORY

"Girl, you're gonna miss homecoming?" Tiana's friend Jasmine blurted out in frustration.

Jasmine and Tiana had gone through so much over the years, from parties to pain,

and Jasmine was not happy that her best friend was going to drop their plans in order to hibernate.

"Like, what does that even mean, sis?" Jasmine continued. "Can't you hibernate later? This is our five year reunion and everyone is going to be there."

Tiana thought she was ready for this hibernation, but Jasmine made some good points. She began to question her decision to withdraw. Did God *really* tell me to hibernate? Maybe God didn't mean right *now*. Perhaps, God was saying eventually, which means I can go to homecoming and be great.

Yes, Tiana thought. *Hibernation can wait.*

As Tiana opened her mouth to reassure Jasmine, she was overcome with clarity. She realized that not only was this right time, but she realized that her friend was one of the pieces she'd have to leave behind. She loved and cherished their friendship, but she finally realized that hibernation means letting go of some things—and maybe some people, too.

APPLICATION

When God calls us to hibernate, it is usually not at a convenient time. The call to hibernate is one that requires that you accept the idea that you may miss out on a few things. As we think through what that really means, it is imperative that we address what we can and cannot bring with us. It requires us to pay attention to who and what we give access to our minds, our hearts, and even our spirits.

Think about what happens to your spirit after you ingest information from certain sources. When you binge-watch reality television, are you more prone to arguments? When you leave girls' night, are you excited about future relationships or do you leave feeling depressed? When you listen to your favorite artist, is your hope restored or do you feel drained? Oftentimes, we overlook the way these seemingly minor aspects of our lives can cause a shift in our spirits, but these are the very things we need to acknowledge.

In order for hibernation to be successful, you must be comfortable with being by yourself. There are people who will not understand, and there will most certainly be times when the fear of missing out tries to draw you out of your hibernation season. In order to stifle that temptation, take some time to think about things or even people that you may need to release so that your hibernation period can be both purposeful and effective.

PRAYER

My God, and my friend, I am so thankful that You have called me to hibernate. I know that You can see beyond where I am and that You have plans for me that are greater than my own. God, I ask in this very moment, as I prepare to hibernate, that You give me clarity as to what I need to give up and what I need to bring with me during this season. Help me to see anything or anyone that might prevent me from embracing this time of withdrawal. God, I want my hibernation to be effective. If there is anything that will block this, PLEASE make it plain. I pray that once You make this known, You might give me the strength to follow-through. Help me to trust in You when I begin to doubt myself. I love You, and I thank You in advance. In Jesus' name, I pray, Amen.

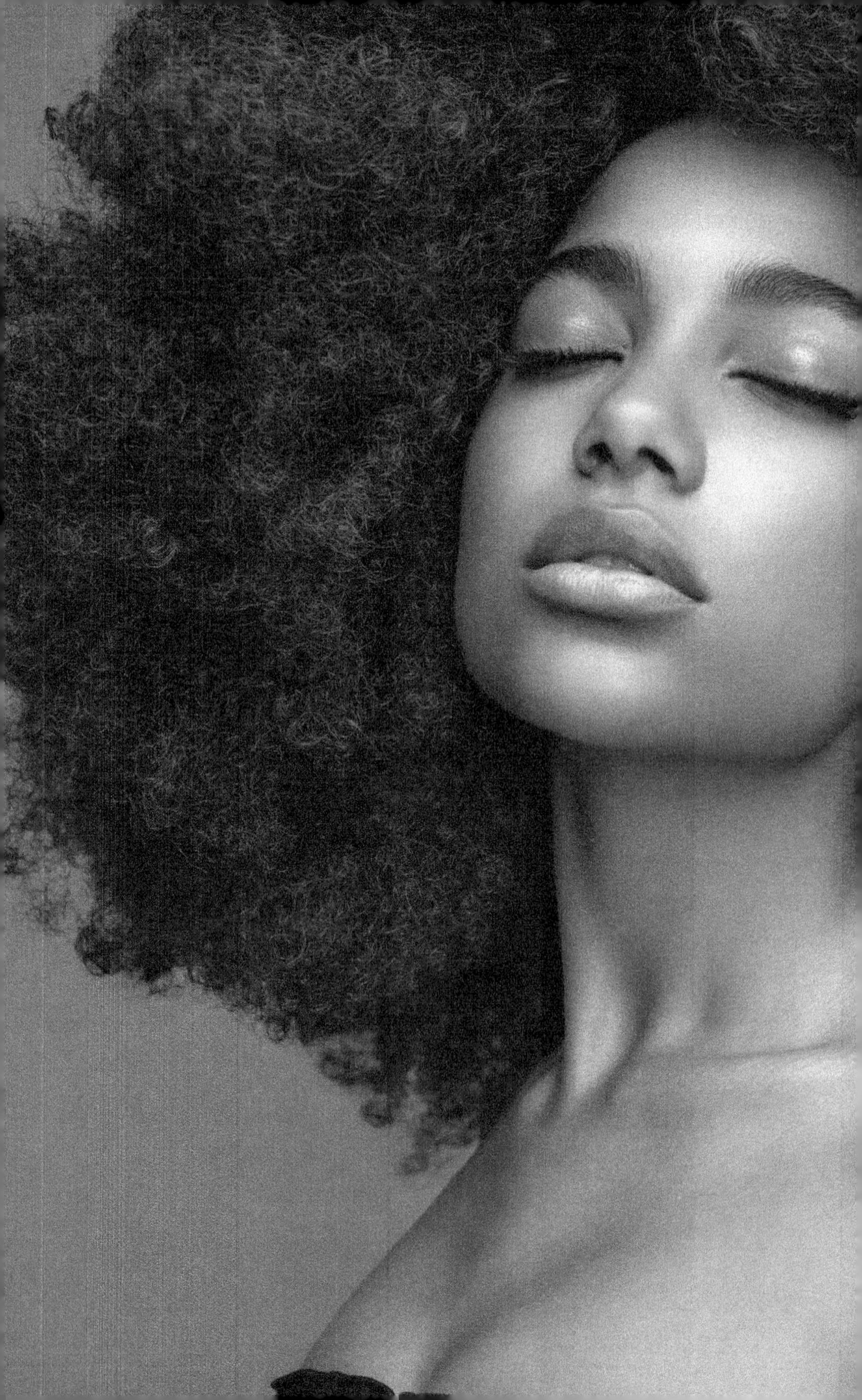

DAY 3
HEAL IN HIBERNATION

What hurts, triggers, or self-sabotaging traits do you need to address in this season of hibernation?

"Turn again, and tell Hezekiah the captain of my people, Thus saith the Lord, the God of David thy father, I have heard thy prayer, I have seen thy tears: behold, I will heal thee: on the third day thou shalt go up unto the house of the Lord."

(II KINGS 20:5)

STORY

Tiana reached for her phone and heaved a melancholy sigh. Eric, her ex-boyfriend, was calling. Immediately, a wave of hurt and regret washed over her as she was reminded of all that she dealt with in their relationship. As Tiana declined the call, she wondered if her hibernation would finally give her the autonomy to mend the brokenness she dealt with on a daily basis.

Over a year ago, Eric had broken her heart and she still had not fully recovered. Her loyalty to the relationship and the deep-seated desire to receive a return on the investment she made in him caused her to allow him back into her life several times. Eric always said the right things, at first. Each time she'd get her hopes up, he would let her down. Here she was again thinking of listening to his lies.

I don't want to be broken forever, she told herself. *If I truly want God's best, I can't be so quick to return to less.* Tiana was reminded that God is near the brokenhearted so she began to look forward to her hibernation.

When the hum of the phone against the desk shifted her attention, she answered.

"Hello," Eric quietly spoke. "Tiana? Are you there?"

"Not anymore," Tiana replied and hung up the phone. She was ready to be restored.

APPLICATION

Once we withdraw from the world and enter our hibernation, we are left with ourselves. This forces us to come face-to-face with anything in us that has held us back or stifled our growth. Now that you are alone, and it is just you and God, what will you discover? Have you fully dealt with the abandonment, the disappointment, the pain? Are you ready to be honest with yourself?

The art of Kintsugi involves broken pottery being put back together with liquid gold. As a result, a piece that was once inconsequential is made more valuable after it has been broken. The key is that the broken vessel had to be brought to a potter who was able to make this possible. Hibernation is a great opportunity to take our brokenness, lay it at God's throne, and trust that He will put us back together. God is able to fill every crack of our brokenness with gold that is worth far more than our human minds could ever imagine.

Please remember that God has sent us therapists and counselors to help us through our hurt. If you feel overwhelmed in this moment, please know that there are options available to you.

PRAYER

My God and my potter, thank You that my brokenness does not have the final say. I thank You that You are still a healer. I thank You that I don't have to allow the pain of my past to define or even shape my future. Today, I lay all my insecurities, my hurt, and my heart at Your feet. I ask that You bind up my wounds. God, please heal me from the scars on the surface and the ones deep within. I know that You understand the language of lament and that You can handle it when I bring my anger, disappointment, and despair directly to You. I thank You for the reminder that even though I may come to You broken, I will leave whole. In Jesus' name, I pray, Amen.

DAY 4
GROW IN HIBERNATION

How will you allow your cocoon to shape you?

"Meditate upon these things; give thyself wholly to them; that thy profiting may appear to all."
(I TIMOTHY 4:15)

STORY

"Grow well, baby girl," Tiana's grandmother said. She was known for her cryptic and often irritatingly brief advice.

For some reason, during Tiana's afternoon walk, her grandmother's words kept popping up in her head. *What does that mean?* Tiana wondered. *Isn't all growth good?*

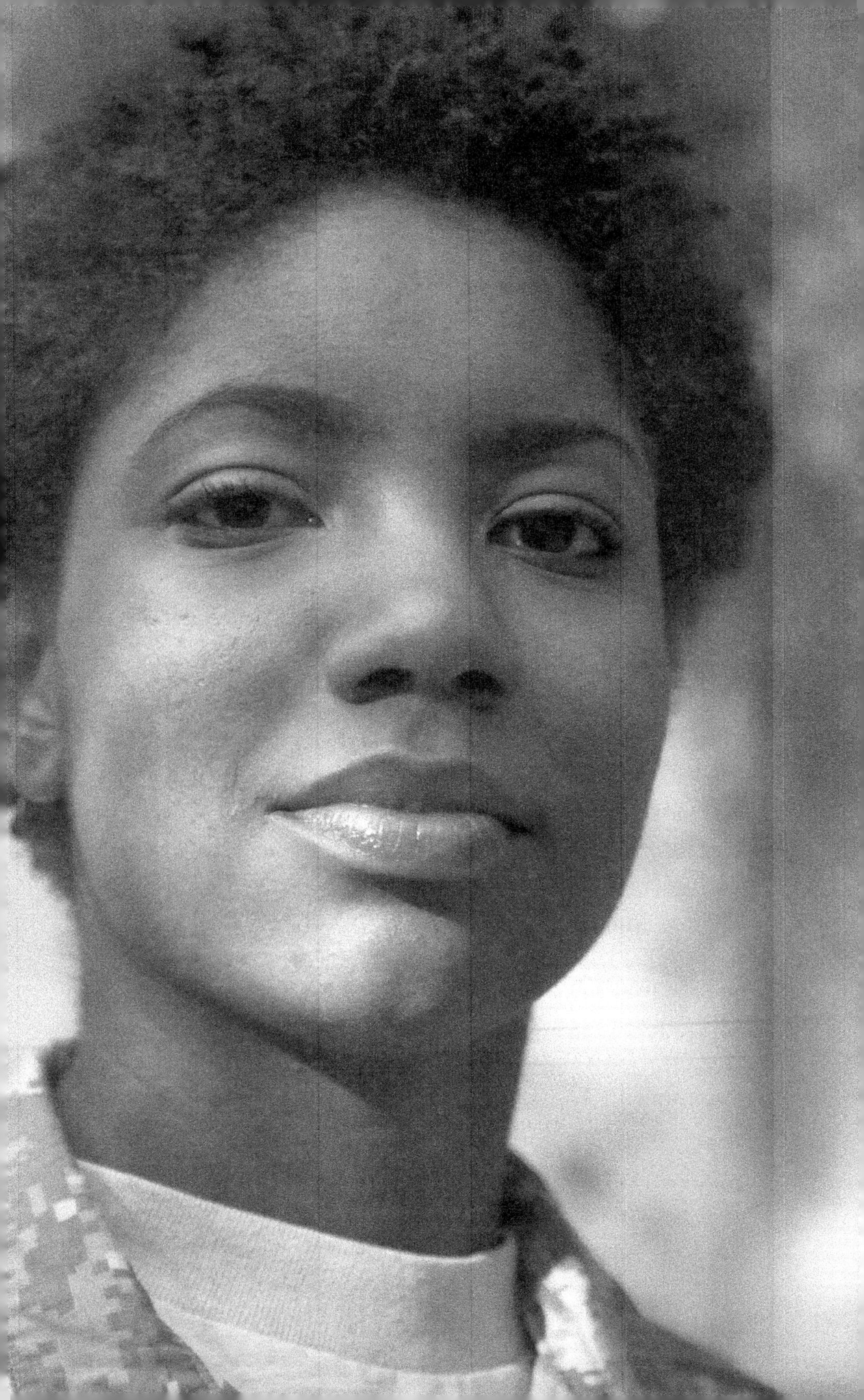

As she continued on her walk, she tripped over a raised sidewalk. Once she dusted herself off (and of course made sure no one cute saw it happen), she realized that the sidewalk had lifted because the roots of the tree alongside it had grown beneath it. Since the tree could not make room for itself, it caused the sidewalk to lift so that it could continue to grow. That lift caused Tiana to stumble.

Tiana wondered if her personal growth would be well-received. Would it cause someone to stumble or falter in their own journey? Or would her growth mesh seamlessly with those around her? How could she grow well?

APPLICATION

Caterpillars are overlooked creatures. They are small, unobtrusive, and depending on whom you ask, really gross. Interestingly, a caterpillar only has two options in its future; it will either become a butterfly or a moth. Both the butterfly and the moth have their place in this world. Yet, one is considered a beauty and the other a nuisance. In our own hibernation, our own cocoon, what will be the deciding factor for our growth? Will we emerge as butterflies or as moths? Will we grow well? We, unlike the caterpillar, have a choice.

The only way to ensure that our growth is a thing of beauty is to do the hard work during our hibernation. We have to prune ourselves to cut off our doubts, our fears, and our shame so that we are left with hope, peace, and confidence. This is a painful process. It is painful because it requires an internal assessment. You have to look inside yourself to see that you are hurting you. What do you do to sabotage yourself? Have you disappointed yourself? Have you forgiven yourself? Do you believe in you? Ask yourself these questions, and then ask God to show you the way He sees you. You are a queen; you are powerful; you are victorious. It is not enough to hear it or read it; you have to believe it about yourself.

Hibernation is the best way to renew your faith in you, and more importantly, renew your faith in God who resides in you. Once this season is over, you will be ready for what God has in store.

PRAYER

God, prune me and shape me during my hibernation so that on the other side of this I will be able to walk confidently into the abundant life Christ came to give me. God, I know this will not be easy, but I am ready. I ask that when I am weak, I might find strength in You. I ask that when I am scared or worried, You might show up and bless me with perfect peace. I ask that You show me how You see me. God, I want to be diligent in this season so that I can be victorious in the next. Have Your will and Your way in my cocoon and in my life. I want to grow well and I trust You with all of me. In Jesus' name, I pray, Amen.

www.urbanspirit.biz

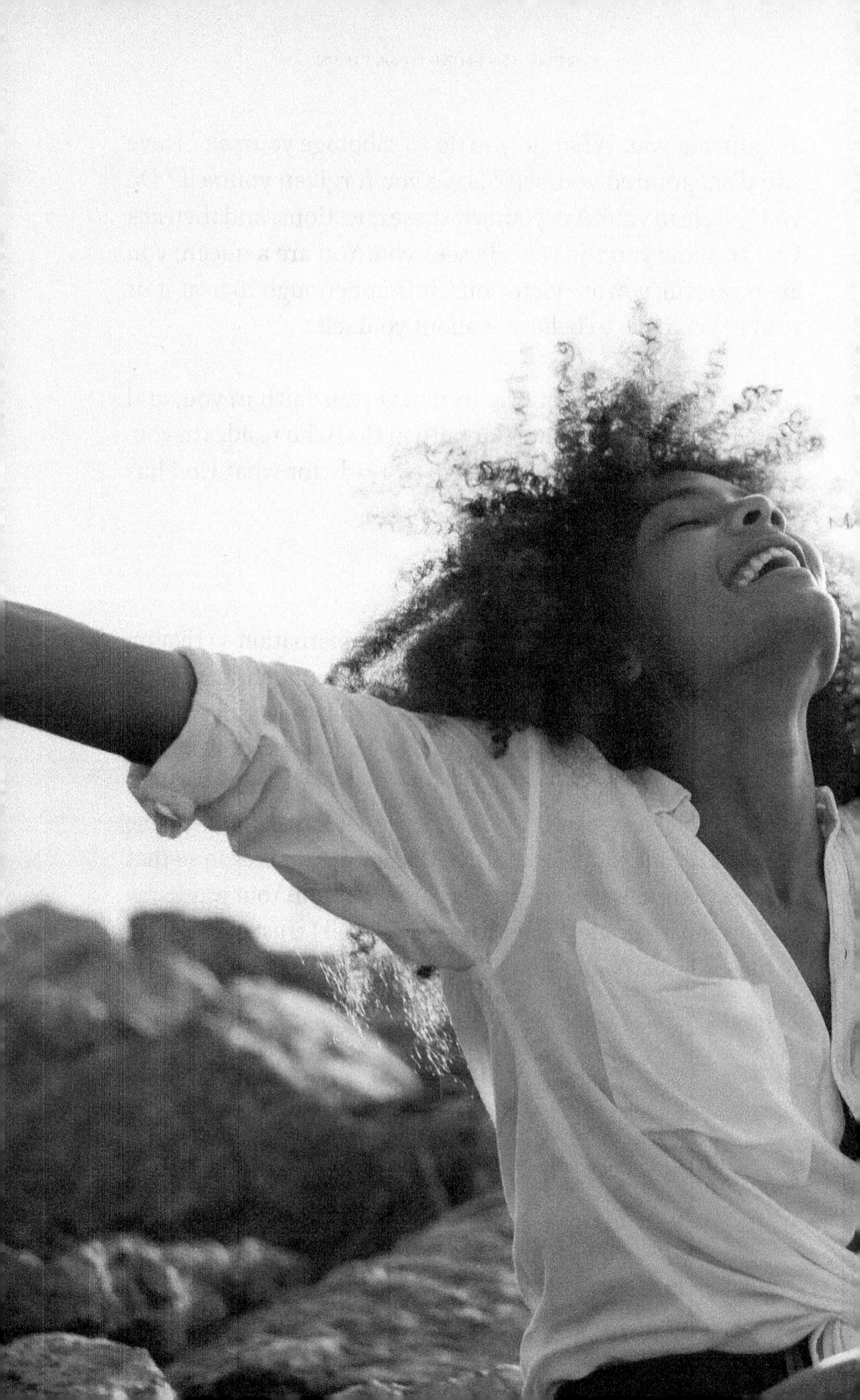

DAY 5
DEPART FROM HIBERNATION

What happens next?

"For I know the thoughts that I think toward you, saith the Lord, thoughts of peace, and not of evil, to give you an expected end."

(JEREMIAH 29:11)

STORY

Tiana began to enjoy hibernation. It was freeing to not be so inundated with social media and the thoughts of others that it was hard to have an organic thought of her own. It was nice to be able to fall in love with herself again and hear from God in a way that is only possible when you quiet the loudness of the world. However, she didn't know if she was she ready to come out of hibernation.

It's comfortable in this space, she thought. *I know who I am here. What if I leave this season and forget again? Am I ready?"*

Suddenly, and as if on cue, Meeko, Tiana's bright-eyed and ever-excited Goldendoodle came bounding up to Tiana's lap with eyes that said, "It's time."

As Tiana grabbed Meeko's leash and prepared to take him outside for his walk, she began to think about all that she was able to accomplish in her hibernation. While there was still work that she needed to do, she finally felt prepared to do it. Her little niece, Ella was waiting at the door to join them on their walk.

"Are you ready, Aunt Ti?" Ella exclaimed.

Tiana watched as Ella and Meeko with enthusiasm. She responded, "Yes Ella, I think I am."

Tiana took a step outside, felt the sun and the crisp clean air on her skin, and realized that not only was she ready to come out of hibernation, but for the first time in a long time, she was excited about her future.

APPLICATION

Once we have embraced, prepped, healed, and grown in our hibernation, the cocoon can begin to feel like a safe space we would rather not leave. Once we have gotten comfortable, it can be very easy to become complacent. We will discover so much about who we are and who God has called us to be that it can be daunting to think about going back into a world

DEPART FROM HIBERNATION

that is so full of brokenness and chaos. Yet, it is important to remember that a hibernation season is meant to be just that—a season. You are *not* meant to stay closed off from the world indefinitely.

You cannot hibernate forever. Eventually, you are supposed to exit this season and walk into the next. Once God has shown you who you are and reminded you of your gifts, He expects you to share your gifts with the world. After all, we need you because you are the only Y-O-U there is. What you were created to do CANNOT be done by anyone else. Even if there are people out there doing exactly what you believe God called you to do, I guarantee that they are not, will not, and could not do it the way that you can. That is why there is an abundance of makeup brands, car models, and clothing lines. Each company, each industry, and each person has a different perspective—and we need yours.

So, don't allow your cocoon to become your coffin. Remember that the God who got you through your season of hibernation will be there to help you win on the other side.

PRAYER

Mighty God, wonderful counselor, and everlasting friend, I am at the end of my season of hibernation and I am unsure of what is next. Thank You for healing my brokenness and for helping me to grow well. While I don't know what will happen once I exit my cocoon, I know that You do. I trust that not only will things work out, but that they will work out for my good. I thank You for doing exceedingly and abundantly beyond anything I could ask, think, or imagine for myself. I am so excited about the next chapter, God, because I know that we are just getting started. God, show up and show out in this next season in the way that only You can. In Jesus' name, I pray Amen.

DECORATE - REV. DR. ROBIN E. WILSON

DECEMBER
WEEK 4

DAY 1
DECORATE WITH PATIENCE

How do you respond to waiting?

"Whose adorning let it not be that outward adorning of plaiting the hair, and of wearing of gold, or of putting on of apparel."
(I PETER 3:3)

STORY

During Sunday morning worship, Lisa listened intently as the litany about the beginning of the Advent Season was read. The invocation focused on the anticipation and longing felt as God's people awaited the promised Savior. Lisa's mind began to drift to her list of desires.

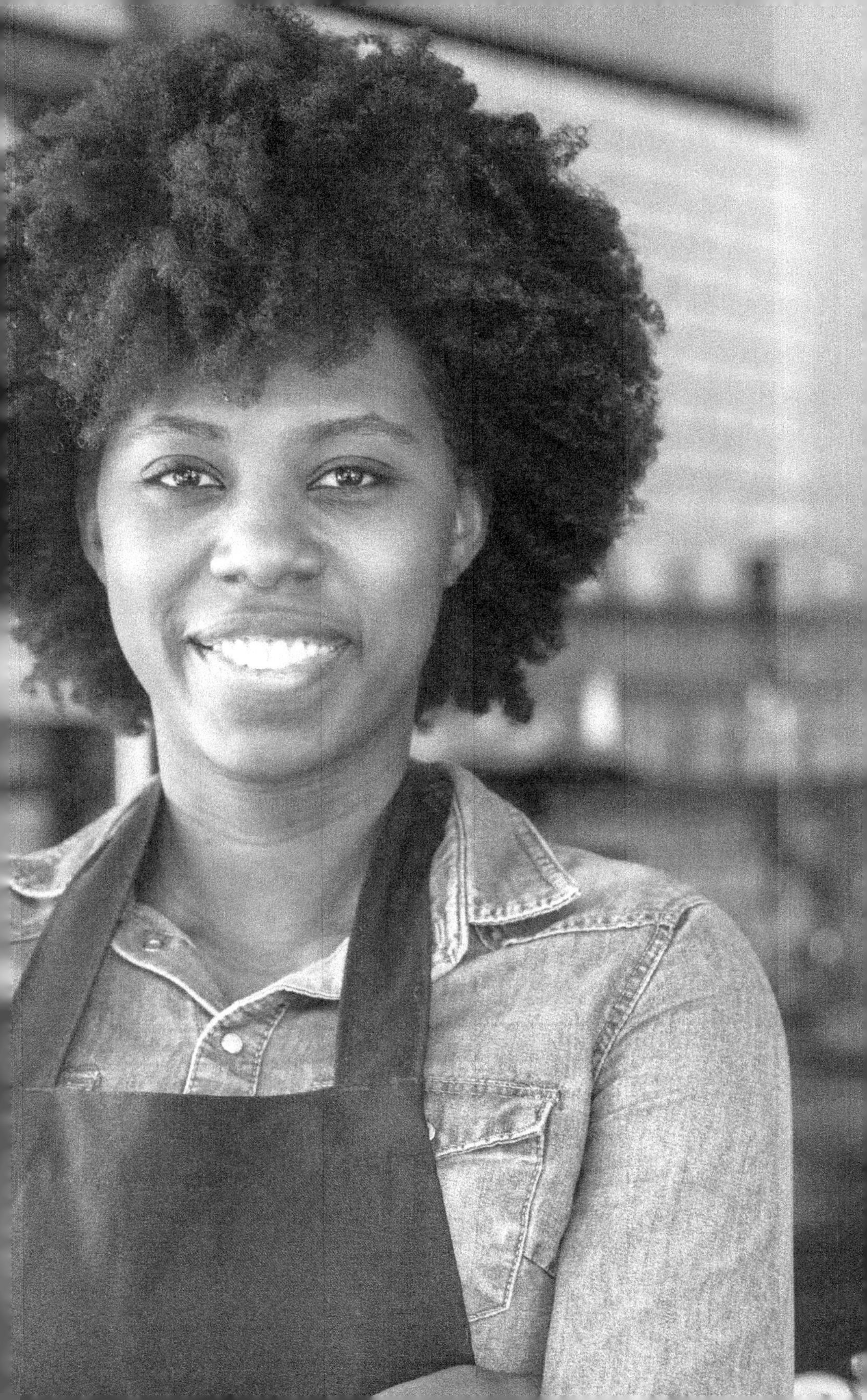

For months, she prayed that a door would open at work, allowing her to make the professional advancement for which she had prepared. Lisa believed that after she completed her master's degree, her supervisor would give her more opportunities for leadership within the department. When this didn't happen, Lisa took her desires to the Lord in prayer.

As weeks and months passed, Lisa grew weary. Her performance at work became lackluster; she still met expectations, but she no longer went above and beyond the call of duty. She stopped volunteering for extra tasks, made no attempts to support others, and limited her interactions with her manager. Not only did work suffer, but Lisa's attendance and involvement at church also began to wane. She felt let down by God.

Eventually, a friend from the Women's Ministry at her church noticed and inquired, "Lisa, you seem different lately? Is everything okay?"

Lisa casually replied, "Yes, I am just tired of being stuck in the same place. I have been praying, and now I am tired of waiting."

APPLICATION

No one ever describes their season of waiting as enjoyable. Waiting on someone or something can make even the most devout Christian grow weary. When we are in a season of waiting, our patience seems to be the first thing to go.

Patience seems to be in even shorter supply during the Advent season. This season highlights the end of the wait for God's people. As we decorate our homes, sanctuaries, and even our outward appearances with the symbols of the Christmas season, we must not neglect our internal adornment. When our prayers seem unanswered and require an extended wait, we must practice patience and draw closer to God.

Although being taunted year after year by her rival because her womb was closed, Hannah cried, refused to eat, and prayed and worshiped God. She patiently and fervently prayed to God that He would bless her with a son. Her prayers caught the priest's attention, who eventually offered a blessing and asked that God grant her request.

Hannah serves as a reminder that God is faithful and His timing is perfect. Instead of retreating from Him during our seasons of wait, we must keep our focus on Jesus. Through our worship, praise, and prayer, our resolve is strengthened, and we can endure.

PRAYER

Dear Lord, thank You for the countless reminders throughout the Bible that waiting on You is never in vain. I trust that every yes and every no from You will work for my good. Help me to endure and adorn me with the patience and resolve needed to worship, pray, and praise while in my season of waiting. In Jesus' name, I pray, Amen.

DAY 2
DECORATE WITH KINDNESS

How do you react when disappointed?

"She openeth her mouth with wisdom; and in her tongue is the law of kindness."
(PROVERBS 31:26)

STORY

As Lisa sat in the drive-thru waiting her turn to order coffee, her heart grew heavier. She was embarrassed by how she responded to her sister when she called to cancel their dinner plans at the last minute.

After weeks of playing taxi to her children, long work days, being up to her elbows in the details for the women's celebration at church, and finalizing a big project at work, Lisa was in desperate need of some fun and relaxation. She acquired a sitter, got her hair and nails done, and bought some new jeans. She had been counting down the hours until their night on the town.

In her haste and disappointment, she did not even allow her sister a chance to explain why she needed to cancel their plans. She was so focused on herself that she just said "whatever" and hung up. Moments later, her sister sent a text apologizing and explaining that her youngest daughter was in the emergency room due to an extremely high temperature.

Lisa felt awful because she let her emotions get the best of her. She did not speak with kindness and love in her moment of disappointment. Instead, she was curt and cold. She was not the best version of herself.

Unfortunately, she could not take back her response. However, she decided to take a hot coffee and her cute new outfit to the emergency room with her sister. She wanted to be present with her as she waited for an update on her niece's condition.

APPLICATION

More times than we would like to admit, we let our emotions get the best of us when faced with disappointment. We react and are often left with regret in our humanness because our disappointment has now impacted another. Disappointments and letdowns are a natural part of life, but God gives us examples of how we should respond in those moments.

www.urbanspirit.biz

Anna, the prophet, was married only seven years before being widowed. She never had children and never remarried. Anna did not focus on what was likely a disappointment and deviation from her plans.

Instead, she spent her life in the temple to serve God and others. Anna chose to focus on what she did have instead of what was missing. Her attention and faithfulness were ultimately rewarded, as she was the first to bear witness to Jesus when Mary and Joseph brought Him to the temple.

Setbacks and letdowns cannot be avoided, but we can use those moments as opportunities to bless and serve in other ways.

PRAYER

Dear Lord, thank You for using women like Anna to show us the appropriate response when we encounter disappointments. I pray that I will be an instrument of grace and kindness to others even when setbacks occur. Guide me through those moments of distress and allow me to glorify You at all times. In Jesus' name, I pray, Amen.

DAY 3
DECORATE WITH FAITHFULNESS

How do you remain faithful to yourself and your life's purpose?

"Whether therefore ye eat, or drink, or whatsoever ye do, do all to the glory of God."
(I CORINTHIANS 10:31)

STORY

Lisa's alarm went off at 4:30 a.m. When she turned over to stop the blaring noise, she quickly asked herself why she had agreed to get up before even the roosters.

She did not spring out of bed as she had planned. Instead, she stayed under

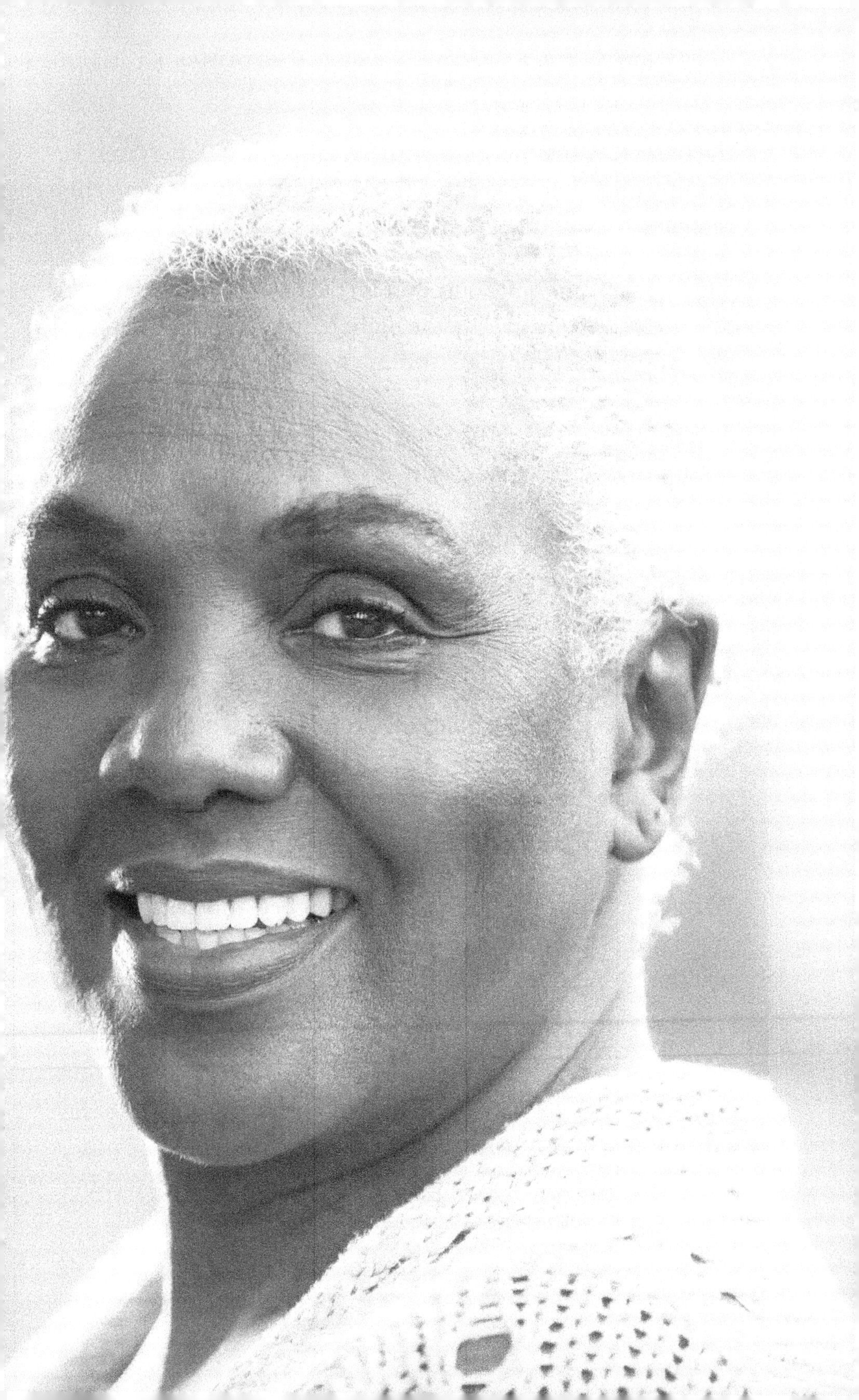

the covers contemplating an excuse she could give her friends, Tammy and Shelia, to explain her failure to meet them this morning for the three mile run.

The excuses came quite quickly. Lisa did have a slight headache. She had worked really late the night before. She was signed up for a yoga class later that evening.

Just as she had settled on what she believed was an acceptable reason to renege on her friends, her phone beeped. The text from Tammy read, "Good morning, Sunshines! I am so thankful for your commitment to helping me reach my wellness goals this year. Meeting you at the gym is a divine appointment. See you in thirty minutes."

That text was just the boost Lisa needed. When she began her fitness journey a year earlier, she promised God that she would be faithful and asked that He use her newfound health as a way to bring Him glory. That chance encounter with Tammy a few months earlier was the answer to her prayers.

With that in mind, Lisa hopped out of bed and said, "Thank You, Lord." No way was she going to falter in her commitment to Tammy, but more importantly, her commitment to God.

APPLICATION

God does not call us to be perfect, but He calls on us to be faithful. Each of us was designed on purpose for a purpose. All of our big and small actions should glorify God by seeking to benefit others rather than ourselves.

DECORATE WITH FAITHFULNESS

Our gifts, talents, and successes are not for us. The glory of God is served when God's people use what they have to bless and benefit others. Remaining faithful to the calling God places on our lives can lead those around us to experience His goodness, mercy, and love.

Think of our lives as walking billboards and testimonies. There is nothing purposeless or insignificant. So when we want to give up or give in, we need only look to our chief designer to be inspired to keep walking in our purpose. If we stay alert, God will send people to remind us.

PRAYER

Father, You are faithful, good, and true. You never fall short on Your promises. Instill in me the same level of faithfulness as I seek to serve and bless others for Your glory. I know that You will equip me to fulfill the purpose for which I was created. Allow me to walk boldly, living out my purpose through this day. In Jesus' name, I pray, Amen.

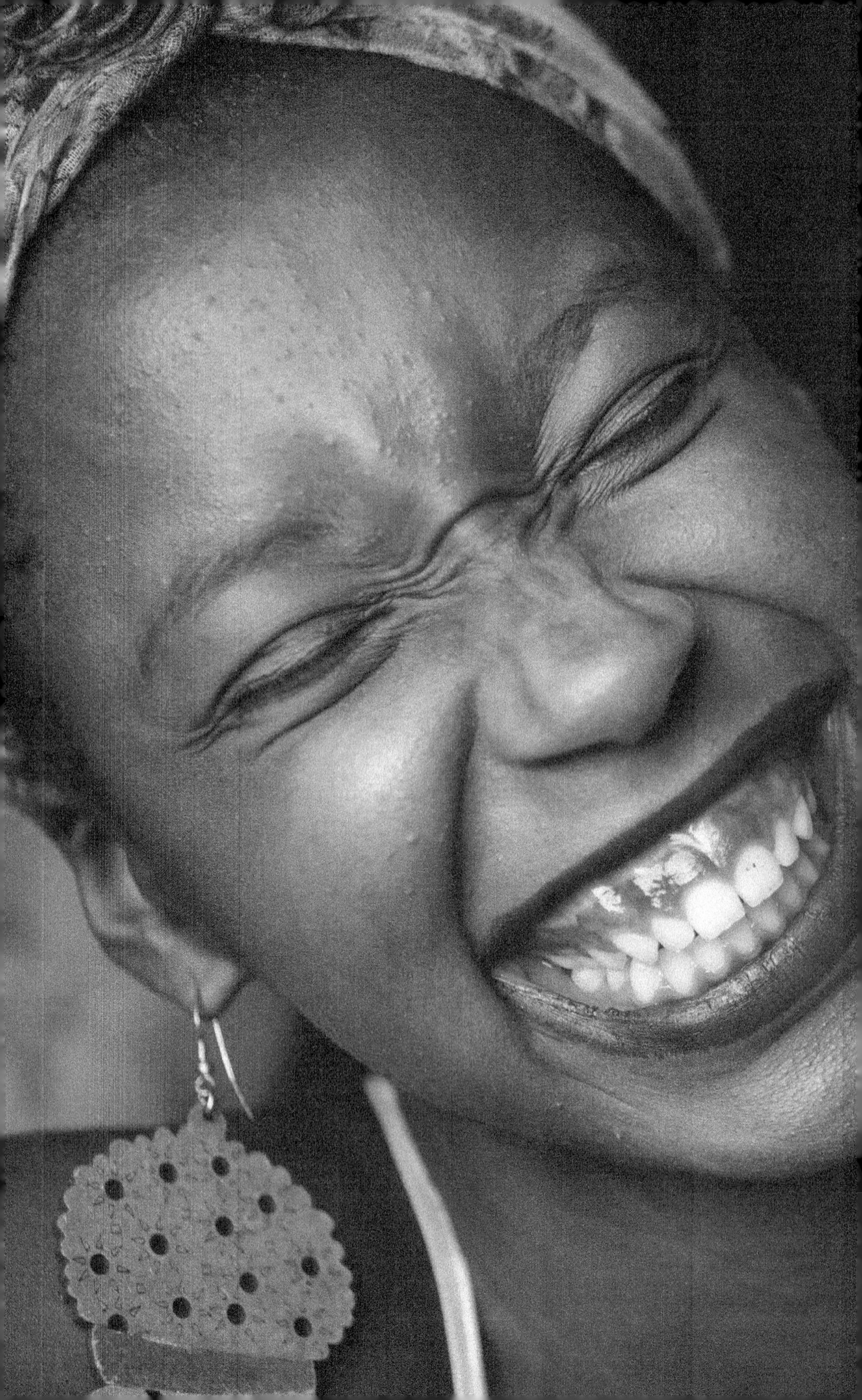

DAY 4
DECORATE WITH JOY

How do you live with joy on purpose?

"My brethren, count it all joy when ye fall into divers temptations; Knowing this, that the trying of your faith worketh patience."

(JAMES 1:2-3)

STORY

Every time Lisa encountered an unexpected setback, she immediately thought of Susan. Susan embodied the idea of choosing joy on purpose.

When their paths crossed, Susan had been recently widowed and was adjusting to life alone in her 2,000 sq. ft. farmhouse that she had shared for over thirty years with her husband. Susan decided that the only way she could keep moving forward was to choose joy on purpose daily.

She found joy by serving others, so she asked God for a divine appointment each morning. Ironically, that's how Susan and Lisa met. Lisa was her divine appointment at a coffee shop on a random Thursday in February. Their divine appointment led to Lisa joining the faculty at the small liberal arts university where Susan had taught for years.

One morning, everyone in their small department noticed something odd. It was 10 a.m. and the door to Susan's office was closed with the light still off. After several attempts to reach her, they all became concerned, paused for a moment of prayer, and then decided they had to call Susan's son. He lived out of state, and the last thing they wanted was to worry him.

Just as their department chair prepared to make the call, the phone rang. It was Susan. She had accidentally closed her hand in the garage that morning. She was sitting in the emergency room waiting for the stitches to be completed.

As Susan recounted the morning events, her voice was jovial and light. She was excited, because thanks to the previous night's snowfall, she immersed her hand in the snow while awaiting the ambulance. This stopped the bleeding and kept her from passing out.

However, she was most excited about the divine appointment in the emergency room. Susan had been able to minister to a nurse who was in the midst of a nasty divorce. Susan saw the pain she had endured that morning as the set up to allow her to alleviate another's pain and share the joy of the Lord. She was elated that God had answered her prayer for a divine appointment so early in the day.

APPLICATION

The Apostle Paul knew precisely what it was to encounter trials in life. He had also handed out his share of tribulations to others. However, when he writes to the Church at Philippi, he reminds us to choose joy. When we are in need, we can choose joy. When we have abundance, we can choose joy.

Paul lets us in on the secret that being joyful in every situation is our reliance on Christ and the strength that comes from Him. We are guaranteed to have challenges in our lives, but we do not have to allow those to dictate our daily disposition. Instead, we can wake up each day and choose our outlook, just like choosing our accessories. We can and should choose joy on purpose.

PRAYER

Dear Lord, thank You for the ability to choose my outlook each day. I ask that You aid me as I seek to choose joy on purpose. Help me be content in any situation, remaining fully confident that You will use each moment to draw me closer to You. I pray for a divine encounter as a way to bless someone else along this journey. In Jesus' name, I pray, Amen.

DAY 5
DECORATE WITH LOVE

How do you demonstrate genuine, unselfish concern for others?

"And above all these things put on charity, which is the bond of perfectness."
(COLOSSIANS 3:14)

STORY

Lisa thought it was odd that blaring through the speakers as she entered her Women's Bible Study were the words, "What's love got to do with it?" Even more bizarre was the fact that just that portion of the song was looping over and over.

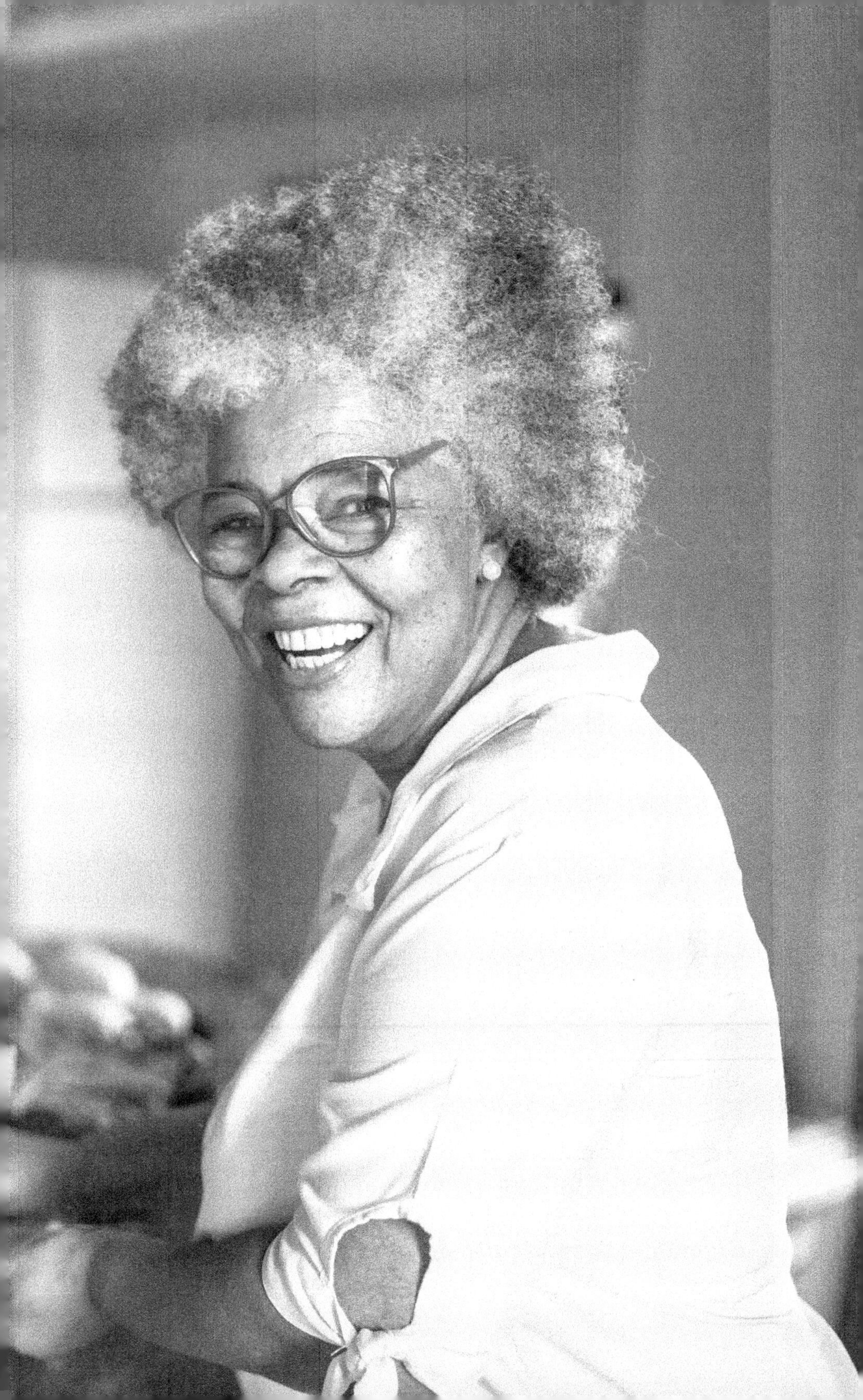

At first, she thought it was a glitch in the system. Then, she quickly realized that Pastor Jessica had done this intentionally.

As Lisa took her seat next to her best friend, Cathy, they chuckled. Cathy then said, "Oh my, what are we in for today? Pastor J is clearly up to something." Shelia nodded in agreement and settled in for what indeed would be a lively discussion.

Pastor Jessica eventually turned the music off and addressed what she knew was on the minds of all twenty of the women who had gathered that evening. She went on to explain that she knew that for the rest of the week, that song lyric would play over and over in each woman's brain. That was her intent. She told them that not only did she want them asking the question, "What's love got to do with it?" but she also wanted them to have the only correct answer. As the women waited on the edge of their seats for the answer, Pastor J paused and took a deep breath for dramatic effect. She then whispered— EVERYTHING!

Once the silence was broken by laughter, and a chorus of "Amen," Lisa and the other women spent the evening examining every facet of their current challenges. It seemed that no matter the struggle that any group member put on the floor for discussion, the answer always came back to love. A love that is only found in Christ. A love that can only be given through the power of Christ.

Before the night was over, anytime someone asked, "What's love got to do with it?" the entire group emphatically responded, "EVERYTHING!"

APPLICATION

The relationship between Ruth and Naomi epitomizes the kind of love we are called to bestow upon others. It is selfless and mimics the type of love referenced in the Gospel of John.

After the death of her husband, Ruth made a commitment to Naomi and to God. Despite Naomi's urging to move on with her life, Ruth declared that nothing but death would separate her from her mother-in-law.

As these two women embarked upon a life together, they discovered that committing to love and blessing another also blesses God. Ruth's willingness to selflessly serve and sacrifice to provide for Naomi led to the biggest blessing in her life.

It is ironic how God works. He gains pleasure in seeing us love one another and bless others. He blesses and loves us back in ways that we could never fathom.

PRAYER

Dear Lord, thank You for the never-ending love You bestow upon me daily. Your grace and mercy remind me that I am called to be an instrument of love to all those I encounter. May my actions exemplify the perfect love that comes from You. I pray that each person I meet today knows they are loved by me, but more importantly, they are loved by You. In Jesus' name, I pray, Amen.

CELEBRATION - REV. DR. BILLIE BOYD-COX

DECEMBER
WEEK 5

DAY 1
CELEBRATION REQUIRES TIME FOR REFLECTION

Do you really have it all together?

"Before I formed thee in the belly I knew thee; and before thou camest forth out of the womb I sanctified thee, and I ordained thee a prophet unto the nations."

(JEREMIAH 1:5)

STORY

Sharra was extremely excited about today's worship service. It was going to be a high time of celebration. This was the day she had prayed for. She felt called to ministry many years ago and today was the day she was being affirmed. She busied herself making breakfast, putting on makeup and gathering her garments for the robing portion of the ceremony. Sharra decided to dress in an outfit that would allow her to wear the necessary undergarments for the afternoon service. She had it all planned out until she realized that she had lost track of time and was going to be unfashionably late for service.

Myesha, noticing her late arrival as she slid into a seat near the rear of the sanctuary, sent a quick text message inquiring about her tardiness, asking her if everything was okay. Sharra was always prompt, always early to everything. She replied detailing the choices she was faced with deciding what to wear and if she was going to view the morning worship service online or in person and simply lost track of time.

APPLICATION

In our hurriedness to have everything perfect, we sometimes lose sight of the things we need the most. Even our efforts to be detail oriented can sometimes be futile. Just when we think we have it all together, life happens and we are faced with the reality that we have missed the mark. Missing the mark does not mean that we have failed or that we are failures; it simply means that we may need to press pause. Pressing pause allows us ample time to survey the surrounding landscape. Often times the landscapes of our lives are filled with unnecessary clutter. Pausing helps us look back, look over, and sort through. This is where the details reside.

Celebration usually requires a time of reflection because nothing just happens. There is normally a series of events necessary for one to declare a time of celebration. It helps if we make time to pause, reflect, and give God thanks before moving forward.

PRAYER

Father, thank You that You are the God of all life and You know every detail about us. Thank You that You knew us before we were conceived and You put Your perfect plan in place for our lives. Help us to slow down enough to embrace Your plan and celebrate Your goodness. Guide us by Your Spirit. We welcome Your presence in our everyday lives. Thank You that You are in the small things as well as the big things and You perfect everything that concerns us. In the name of Jesus, I pray, Amen.

DAY 2
CELEBRATION MAKES TIME FOR DIRECTION

What are you going to do now?

> "The steps of a good man are ordered by the LORD: and he delighteth in his way."
> (PSALM 37:23)

STORY

Myesha texted again to update Sharra on the announcements that she missed earlier. "The afternoon service has been moved up one hour to 2 p.m. Free food will be available immediately following service and all celebrants must be dressed and in place by 1:30 p.m. If you have your garments

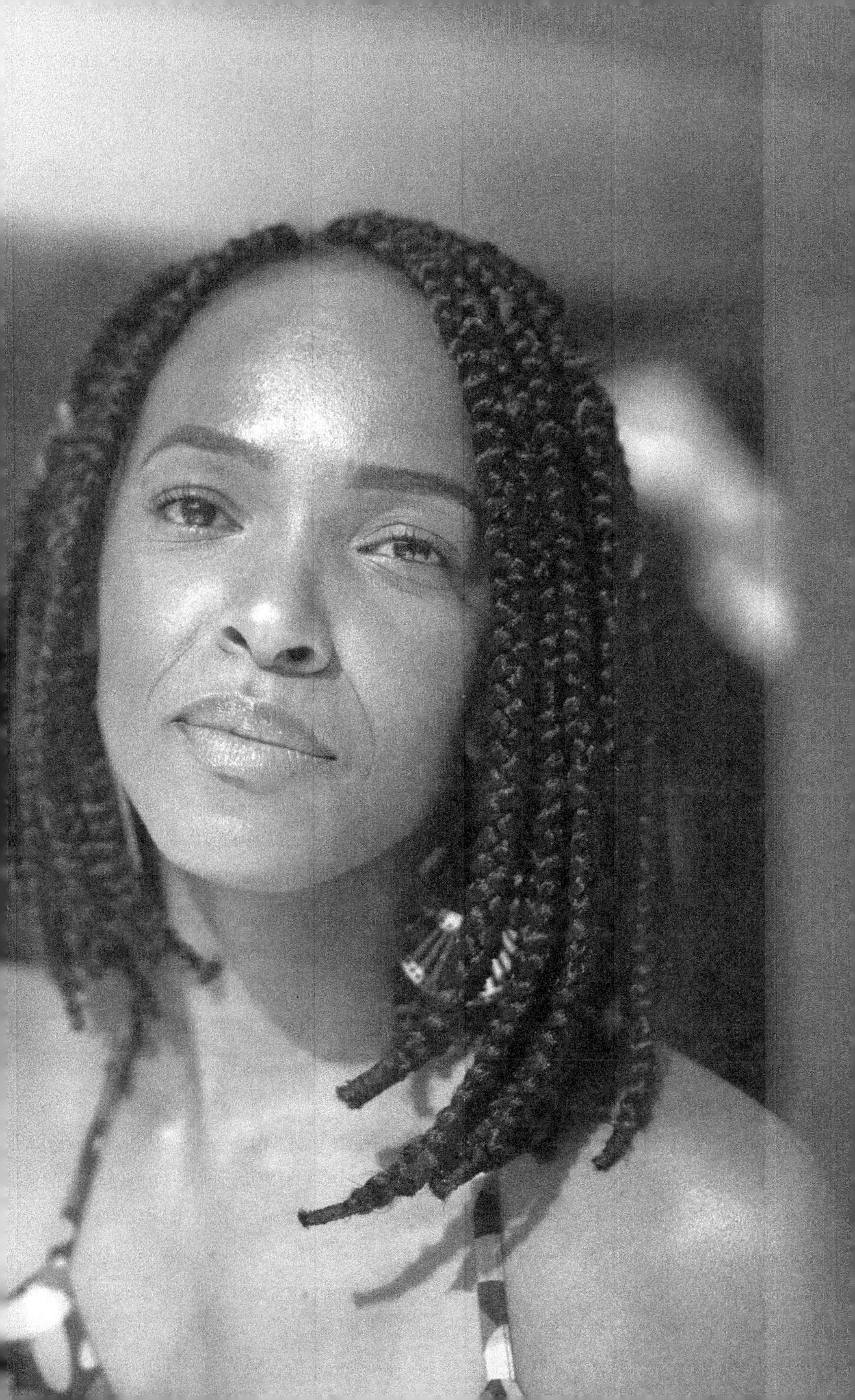

with you, we can grab a quick bite here instead of going off campus.

"Sure, sounds like a plan," Sharra quickly replied.

"I'm glad we didn't have to leave to find food," Sharra sighed. "I've got just enough time to get dressed and in place. We have assigned dressing rooms and I need to make sure that my robe didn't get wrinkled in my car. Myesha, do you mind helping me get dressed? I just need to slip my robe on and change shoes."

"Slip your robe on? That's not how it's done here. You need a black suit or dress for the processional. Didn't you know?"

"OMG! No. I forgot to ask for clarity on the requirements. I made the assumption that I would process in wearing my robe and the other garments would be added during the service. I only have my undergarments. I didn't bring anything else to wear. Lord, what am I going to do now?"

APPLICATION

Life seems good when it appears that things are going your way. That is until you discover you missed a step along the way or you find yourself swimming upstream. In times like these, our first reactions are usually fear and doubt. While these are normal reactions, we don't have to give in to them.

These are the times that we need God the most. We need His grace, which He extends to us freely. We may not have it all together, but we serve a God who knows all and will guide us along life's highways. We have a very present help in the time of trouble. We just need to reach for Him.

We need to talk to God. He is a good loving Father who always wants what is best for His children. He calls us the apple of His eye. He searches the world seeking ways to show Himself strong on our behalf. He is always just a prayer away.

PRAYER

Father, thank You for Your tender mercies and Your saving grace. Thank You for making ways when there seems to be no way. Thank You for knowing my steps before one of them is made. You are the answer to every prayer. You are my stabilizer in good times and hard times. I can run to You and find shelter from the storms of life. Father, guide me in the way You would have me to go. In the name of Jesus, I pray, Amen.

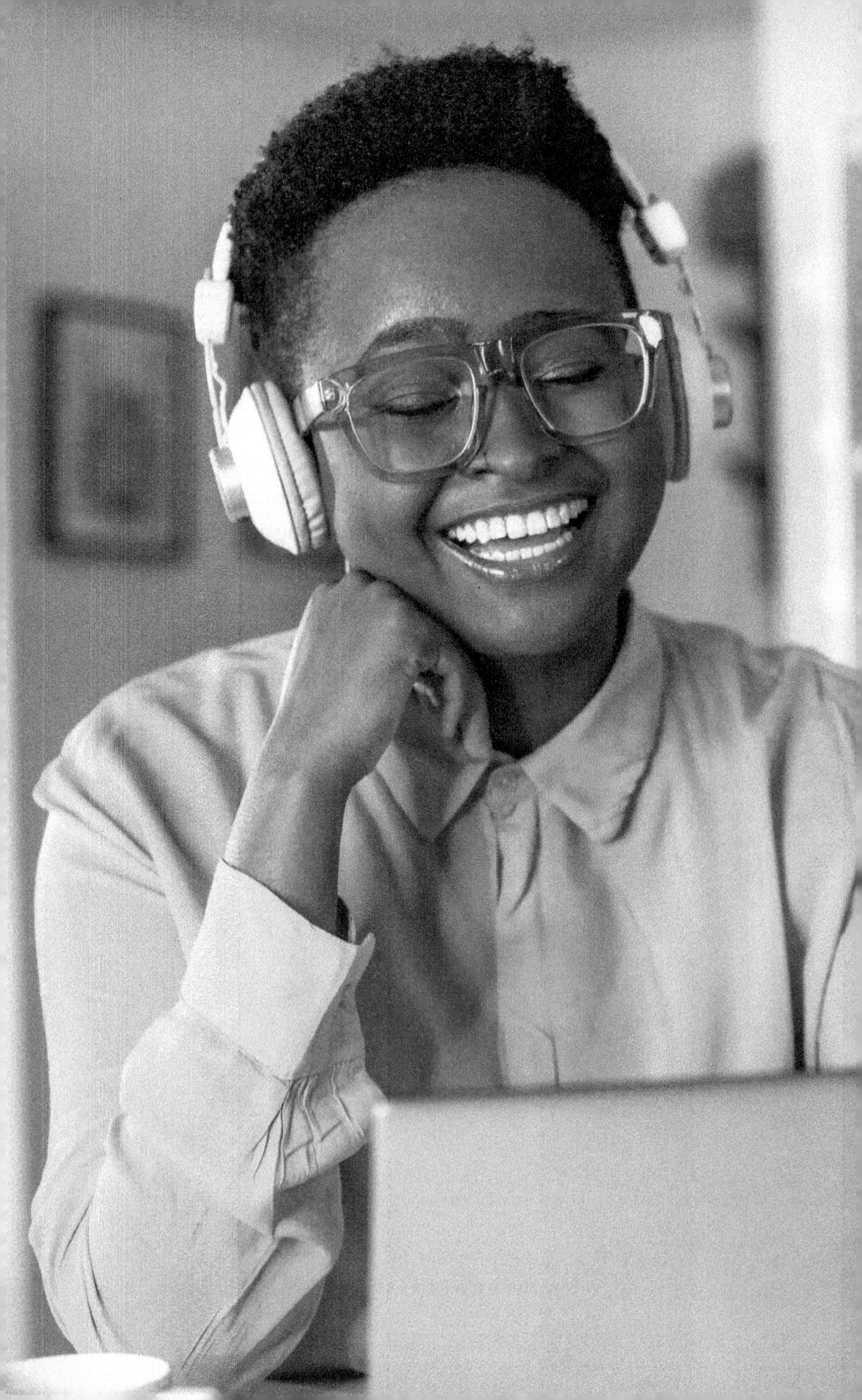

DAY 3
CELEBRATION DEMANDS TIME FOR PROVISION

What other options do you have?

"But my God shall supply all your need according to his riches in glory by Christ Jesus."
(PHILIPPIANS 4:19)

STORY

"I don't know what else to do," Sharra sighed. "I may just need to sit this one out or ask for an exception to wear my robe in. I have no idea how this is going to turn out. I'm scared. I live too far away and I don't know anyone local that can lend me a dress.

I should have followed up with the office. This is my fault. I've waited so long for this day; I can't believe I've come this far and now this."

"Guess what," Myesha said. "I brought a black dress with me this morning and it's hanging right over there. I don't know if it will fit, but anything is worth a try at this point. Since I'm not required to change, I don't mind keeping on this outfit. Let's see if it will work for you."

APPLICATION

Sometimes situations come to redirect, correct, establish, or to shift us. There is always a lesson to learn. Sometimes those lessons come in us in the midst of panic or crisis. Crisis helps us to see God as our faithful provider. He always has a ram in the bush. He is looking for ways to show Himself strong on our behalf. God is in the smallest of details. God cares about everything that concerns us. When we open up to Him, He comes in to provide what is needed.

He knows our needs before we are aware that there is one and He stands at the ready to supply them. God makes sure that what we need is in place when the need is realized. It is not on the way; it is already there because our loving Father is our provider. Our role is to trust Him in all things and talk to Him about everything. His plan is without fault or failure. When we walk along His perfect path, there is no lack. Every resource for every need is there; we just need to look for it and listen to those whom God sends our way.

www.urbanspirit.biz

PRAYER

Father, thank You for being Jehovah Jireh, the Lord our provider. Thank You for the lessons learned in the fires of life. Thank You for not leaving Your plans for me in my hands. Thank You for orchestrating my life before the world began. You already had everything necessary for my life lived already in place. Thank You for establishing my path. In the name of Jesus, I pray, Amen.

DAY 4
CELEBRATION GIVES TIME FOR OBSERVATION

What are you overlooking?

"He maketh me to lie down in green pastures: he leadeth me beside the still waters."
(PSALM 23:2)

STORY

"Oh my goodness, Myesha. It's a perfect fit," Sharra said with a smile. "The dress looks like it was made just for me. What would I have done without your willingness to sacrifice your plans to make sure I am following proper protocol? I would have

been so embarrassed and disappointed if I could not participate in the ceremony. You, my dear friend, are a life saver. I will be forever grateful to you! Years from now as I reflect back on this day, I will tell our story."

"I don't know why I didn't think of it when you first mentioned that you only had the undergarments," Myesha responded.

"It was all in God's timing," replied Sharra.

"This situation has been a great lesson for me," Sharra admitted. "I'm always rushing through life trying to get from point A to point B in the fastest time possible. All of that rushing has caused me to miss the small but equally important things."

APPLICATION

Each day we wake up with the same amount of time as everyone else, twenty-four hours. It is how we spend those hours that matters most. Most days, we speed right through them without taking time to stop and look around us. We allow our to-do lists to control our steps and order our day. When we do this, anything is subject to happen. God is a strategist. He left nothing pertaining to our lives undone. God is in all of the minute details of our lives. He has already perfected everything that concerns us, but we have to slow down to reap the benefits of the preparation.

When we fail to stop, we miss the beauty of creation. We miss God in all the ways that He shows up for us each and every day.

We miss His presence and sometimes His provisions. However, when we slow down and start our day in prayer, we find the wisdom to proceed differently.

PRAYER

Father, Thank You for being the keeper of time. Help me to use it wisely so that I don't miss Your hand at work in my life. Thank You for allowing us to slow down and be restored in Your presence. Thank You for leading us to the place where You draw out of us what is needed and filter through what is unnecessary. We need You to refill us with what is necessary for the next steps on our journey. In the name of Jesus, I pray, Amen.

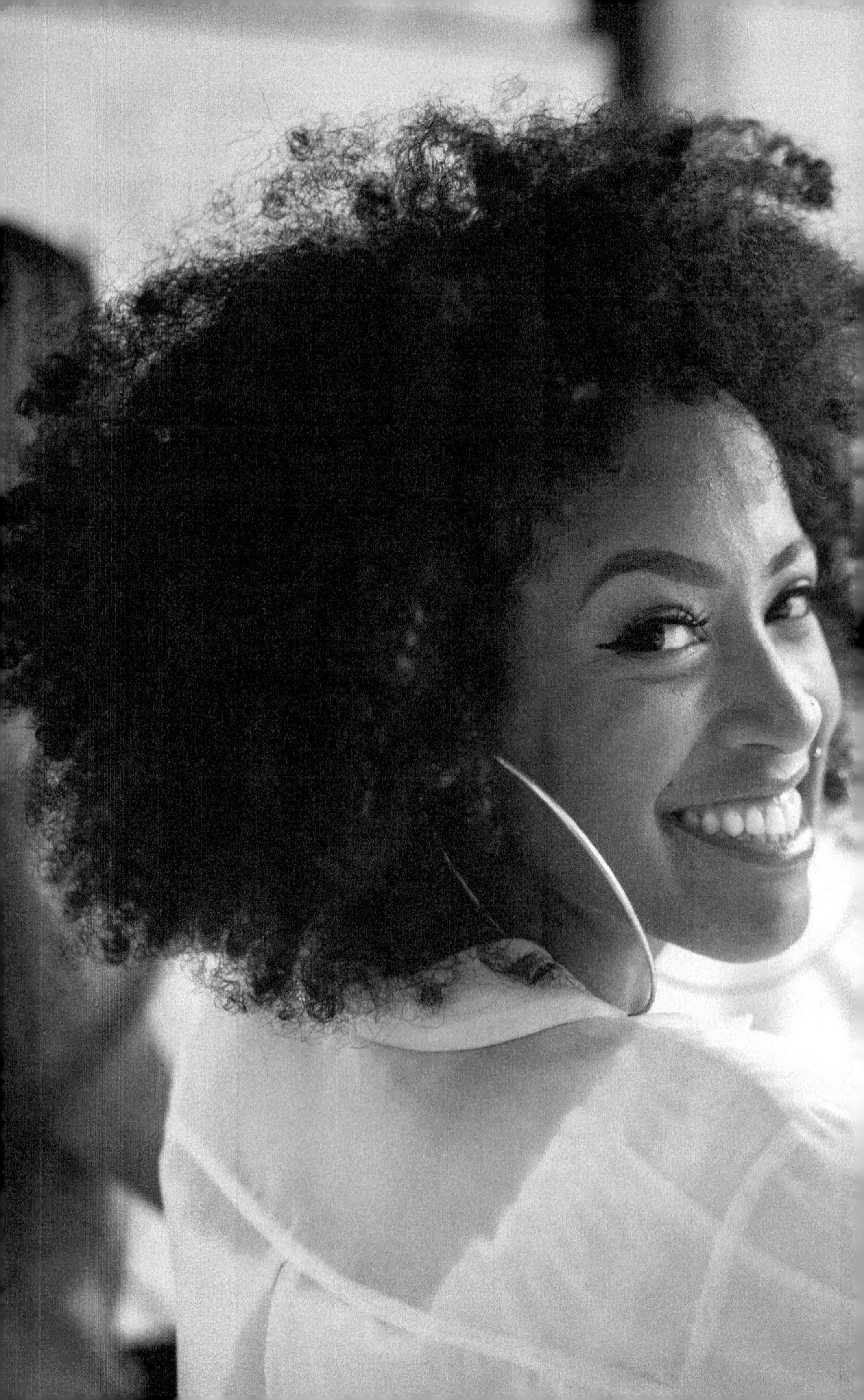

DAY 5

CELEBRATION CREATES TIME FOR CONGRATULATIONS

Aren't you glad you didn't give up?

"And the women answered one another as they played, and said, Saul hath slain his thousands, and David his ten thousands."

(I SAMUEL 18:7)

STORY

"Oh Sharra, I am so proud of you and this major milestone in ministry," said Myesha. "I know how long you have prayed about this and now it's here. I couldn't be happier for you. I see so many great things in your future. You are an awesome teacher, preacher, and a compassionate leader. You are truly an asset to the Body of Christ."

"Thanks friend," Sharra replied. "You have encouraged me so many times when I felt like throwing in the towel. You motivated me and pushed me to keep moving, to keep doing the work. I celebrate you today as well because you have been such an integral part of my spiritual development. You have modeled ministry before me. I have watched you from afar and I have experienced your teachings up close. You, my sister, are amazing!

APPLICATION

As you rise, never forget to reach back and straighten your sister's crown. None of us can reach our destinies alone. We all need someone who will walk this journey with us. Sometimes, we need them to walk in front to show us the way. Sometimes, we need them to walk beside us to help strengthen us. Sometimes, we need them to walk behind us to keep pushing us forward when we do not have the strength or desire to keep moving. Sometimes, we need them to help us slow down to see what we may be missing.

When God places those people in your life, don't forget to celebrate them. Your victory is also their victory. On the cross next to Jesus was another person who was also about to be crucified. There on the cross, he received an invitation from Jesus to share in the beauty of a life in Heaven. Don't forget those around you; when you go up, take someone else with you.

PRAYER

Father, Thank You for making all things beautiful in Your time. I am grateful for those women You have intentionally placed along the highways of my life. You have given some the assignment to go the distance and others are assigned to journey only for a season. Thank You for each of them and for those who are yet to come. I pray that as You have blessed me that You will also bless my sisters. In the name of Jesus, I pray, Amen.

WONDER – KAYLA MONROE

JANUARY
WEEK 6

DAY 1
WONDERS OF THE MIND

Will He leave me?

"Seek the Lord and his strength, seek his face continually. Remember his marvellous works that he hath done, his wonders, and the judgments of his mouth."
(I CHRONICLES 16:11-12)

STORY

"Enough," Margo screamed out of frustration at Rue from across the kitchen table. "This has been the third argument this week that has ended in tears and its only Tuesday!"

Meet Ruby and Marjorie Buckman, better known to the world as Margo and Rue for

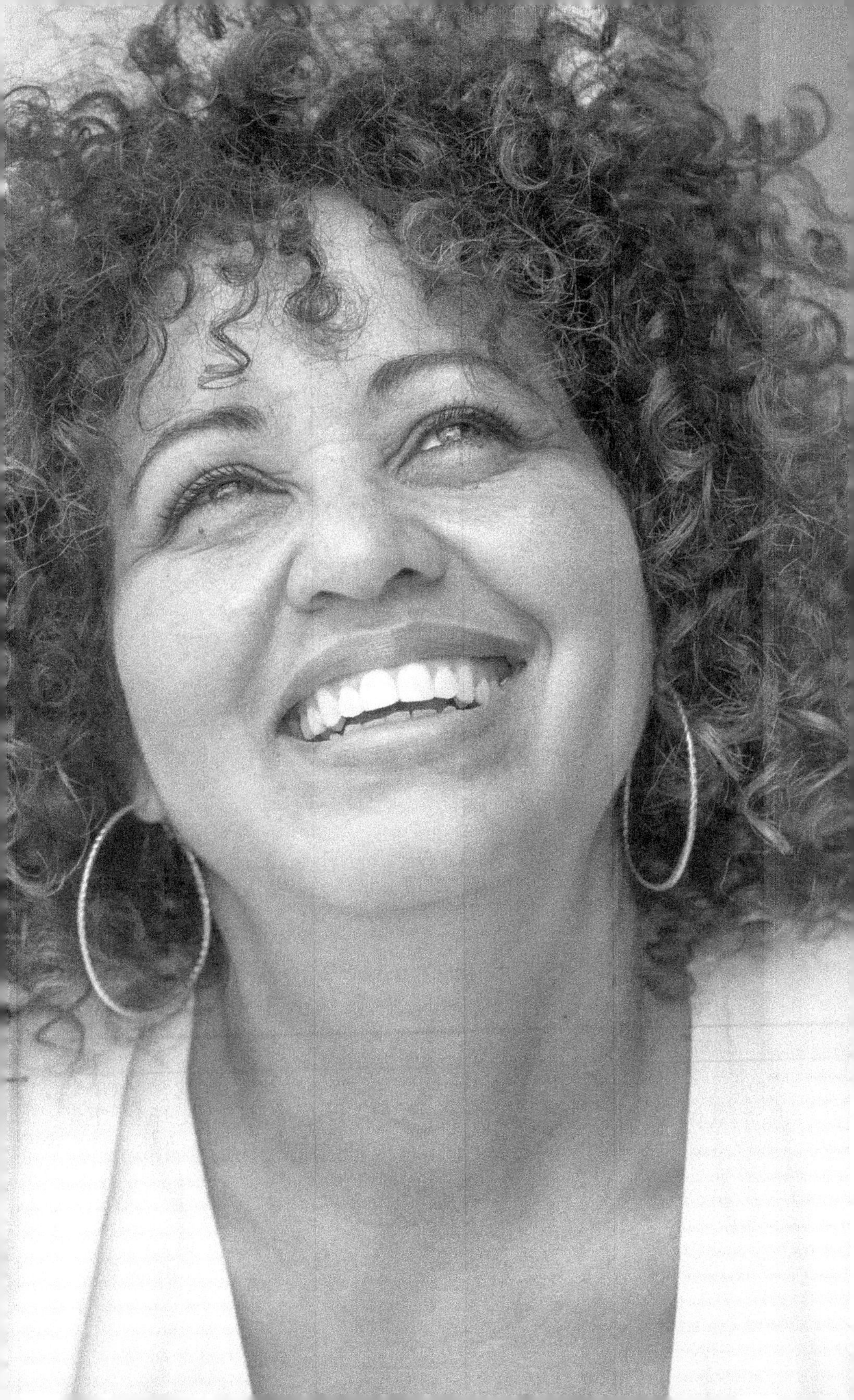

short. The two sisters bickered so much that one would think they were related by blood, but the Buckman sisters met at ages five and seven because their adopted mother could not have one without the other. At least that was how Margo explained the story to Rue. Margo, being the eldest by two years, never let Rue out of her sight.

The two sisters were now seventeen and nineteen years old, and Margo was home for winter break from her sophomore year at UConn while Rue had been stuck in her head all break because the *perfect* sister was back.

"Ouch," Rue squealed as the pillow that Margo catapulted across the room landed in her lap!

"Are you done glazing over the HBCUBuzz Instagram page yet or what?" Margo teased her. Per usual, Rue answered her question with an elongated eye roll—a classic Buckman sister move.

"Get out of your head" was the phrase that Margo set for herself as her New Year reminder goal. In the midst of her, she had had difficulty doing that. All their lives, Rue and Margo had tried to live up to their sister promise of *"No backward steps."* As of late, it seemed that the only steps Margo took were gliding backward.

There were many factors that played into their sister pact. For one, the environment they were born into and the one they grew up in were like night and day. From an early age, the two girls recognized what it took, a miracle really, for them to live the life they lived.

"Remember our phrase? No backward steps Marjorie!" Rue coyly whispered into her sister's ear as she danced out of the living room and back into the kitchen.

Margo just sighed and smiled because Rue could always tell when Margo had begun to let her mind wander. It was weird to the sisters how in sync they found themselves to be, especially when one doubted her ability to do something. The first time they realized that they shared this telepathy was when the two sisters first met. Marjorie was the shy and reserved one, while Ruby was the outgoing and boisterous one. One night, the girls were preparing for bed and Rue overheard someone bullying Margo for still sleeping with her stuffed animal Mr. Peppers.

"Leave her alone," Rue whisper-shouted at the other orphanage kids.

"What are you going to do about it," the kids inquired with a harmonic tone.

As Rue began to charge toward the three girls, they threw Mr. Peppers up in the air. She caught him and returned him to Margo. That night, the two sisters prayed together that they would stick together through whatever life hurled at them. This was also that night that Rue learned why Margo cherished Mr. Peppers. Margo struggled with a whirlwind of anxious thoughts every night as soon as her eyes closed. She explained to Rue that Mr. Peppers helped ease the scary thoughts.

"Grab my hand," Rue whispered to Margo.

Margo quickly reached for Rue's hand under the blankets as Rue began to pray aloud. In that moment, Margo knew that God had sent Rue to be her guardian angel.

APPLICATION

Have you ever had the feeling that God left your side? You know the feeling where it doesn't feel as if your situation could get any worse, and yet it does. If this happens, the first thing to do is inhale and exhale. Then tell yourself, "Everything will be okay." The best part of being in our low moments is that they give us an opportunity to reflect on our decisions and the choices that we made which led to that place.

Remind yourself that God is still in the miracle-making business. All we simply must do is have the faith the size of a mustard seed that we can have anything we want if it is in His will. Often, we lose sight of our faith because we throw ourselves into a whirlwind of thoughts. We ask, "If God is good, why does He leave?" Well, He never leaves. Encourage yourself to review the series of events that landed you where you are currently and begin to thank Him in advance for the valley. God is getting ready to pull you out.

PRAYER

Dear Lord, please show me that You are still with me. I thank You for never forsaking me, and I ask that You shift my mindset to allow room for growth and understanding of my current circumstance. I know that You are a purposeful God, and that everything that happens in our lives is already written in our story. Continue to guide my thoughts from worry to wonder and cover them with Your over abundant love. Thank You for loving me in my low moments as much as You love me in my elevated moments. In Jesus' name, I pray, Amen.

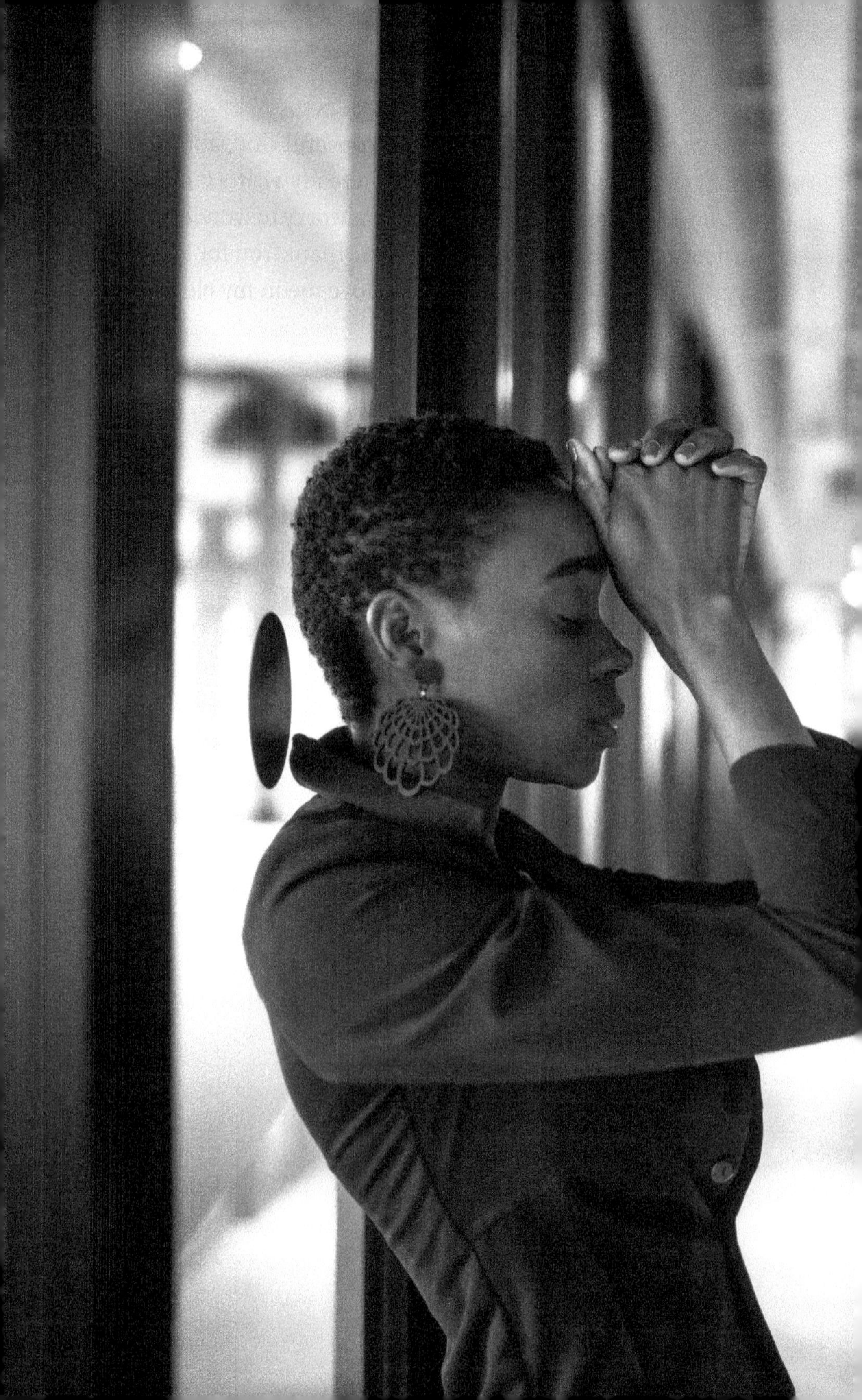

DAY 2
WONDERS OF THE BODY

Will He heal me?

"Is any sick among you? let him call for the elders of the church; and let them pray over him, anointing him with oil in the name of the Lord: And the prayer of faith shall save the sick, and the Lord shall raise him up; and if he have committed sins, they shall be forgiven him."

(JAMES 5:14-15)

STORY

Being in a hospital bed and unable to move her left leg without assistance was not how Margo envisioned the start of the spring semester. The day before when it was time to pack up the car to return to UConn, their mother had noticed Margo moving slower than usual to get out of bed. She was the early riser, and always had a cup of tea and breakfast with her mother every morning. Rue was the complete opposite. She could care less about whether she ate breakfast, let alone taking time to sit down and wait for tea to steep to perfection.

"Ruby, wake up! Go check on your sister because she's not down here yet," their mother hollered from the bottom stairwell.

"Okay, Ma. I heard you the first time!" Rue replied as she shuffled herself out of her cozy blanket to go down the hall to Margo's room. As she slowly dragged herself down the hall singing Margo's name, she thought it was weird that her sister had not told her to shut up already.

Rue knocked and leaned her head into the room. "Hey, Ma was wondering why you skipped out on tea and breakfast this morning, are you okay?" she asked.

Margo let out a deep sigh of pain and struggle that Rue had never before heard come from her sister. Putting Margo and weak in the same sentence was something she couldn't even fathom.

"What's going on?! What's wrong?!" Rue asked with panic in her voice. "Marjorie Michelle, talk to me right now!" Rue frantically flung the door open and hastily ran across the room to her sister's side.

"I don't know Rue, I don't know," Margo responded with tears in her eyes. I've been trying to get up and use the bathroom for the last three hours, but I can't seem to move my left leg at all. Get mom, now!"

"Mom! MOM! Mom, hurry up!" Rue repeatedly cried out.

Both of their parents could sense the urgency in Ruby's voice and ran up the steps, skipping them by two to get there faster. After dialing 911 for assistance, Rue rode with her sister in the ambulance as their parents trailed them to the nearest hospital.

"It's going to be okay; you're going to be okay," Rue kept saying through her tears as she vigorously rubbed the top of Margo's hand.

When everyone reached the hospital, the family was by Marjorie's side as she awaited the results of the multitude of tests. Six different tests later, the doctors were still drawing a blank as to what was causing the paralyzing effect within her left leg.

During her eighty-fifth cry session of the day, Margo was finally ready to see family members outside of her parents and Rue. Both of their grandmothers, Brenda Joyce and Hatterine (affectionately known as Branny and Grandma), had come into town to check on their eldest granddaughter.

"Bran and Gram," Margo cheerfully greeted her grandmothers with the largest grin Rue had seen since her sister had been in the hospital.

"Hi Babygirl," they simultaneously sang to her as they melted into Margo's arms. Ruby dragged two extra chairs up to Margo's bedside.

"We're here to break you out!" Branny jokingly said.

"I wish!" Margo replied gloomily.

"Did you forget what type of grandmothers we have?" Rue questioned her sister.

"The praying kind," both Buckman sisters answered in chorus within seconds of the question.

A few weeks after the grandmothers paid Margo a visit, she was discharged from the ICU and sent to inpatient rehab. Of course, Rue had a million and one jokes because Margo had to rely on a walker with two bright tennis balls decorating the back two legs to carry her to her various destinations.

In her moments of what seemed like loneliness, when all her visitors vanished, Margo reflected on the miracles of God. The doctors still could not tell her exactly what happened and how it happened, but they were able to drain the infectious fluid out of her hip joint to allow her to begin to rebuild the muscle and usage of her left leg again. She knew that this was the apparent work of her grandmothers' prayers over her combined with her faith in God to allow Him to heal her in His time.

APPLICATION

Do you often find yourself asking God, "Why me?" or "How did I get here?" If so, you should know that this is normal. Trust me. What we learn in the Bible, time and time again, is that God will give His greatest battles and tests to His strongest soldiers. Often, it may seem like we can't handle another test, even if it's the size or duration of a pop quiz. These are the times when we must lean on our faith. God knows how easy it is for us to fold and give in to the temptation to give up!

Don't give up! Stay strong in knowing that in our deepest sorrows, God hears our prayers and will acknowledge our obedience of still praising Him amid the storm. Our faith is what holds us together until God delivers His promised miracles. He will always grant us the desires of our hearts when they align with His will.

Lean in, He's still in the healing business!

PRAYER

Dear Lord, when the enemy begins to attack my body, I pray that You remind me that I only need faith the size of a mustard seed for You to heal us. Continue to cover me daily in Your blood from the top of my head to the crown of my feet. Keep me mindful of staying the course in worshiping even when I am under attack. I know that You are a God of many signs and wonders, so when I do feel an attack on my physical, I ask for immediate deliverance from the enemy. Do not allow that weapon to form and prosper. If it is in Your will, I pray that You will minimize it to not prosper within me. Thank You for keeping me in good health! In Jesus' name, I pray, Amen.

DAY 3
WONDERS OF THE SPIRIT

Will He forget me?

"He maketh the storm a calm, so that the waves thereof are still. Then are they glad because they be quiet; so he bringeth them unto their desired haven."

(PSALM 107:29-30)

STORY

"Okay, but literally EVERYONE has a special talent in this family except me!" Rue shouted from the top of stairwell.

"That's far from the true," Margo responded.

Since they were kids, Rue always felt like she came second to her older sister Margo. Even before they became the Buckman Sisters

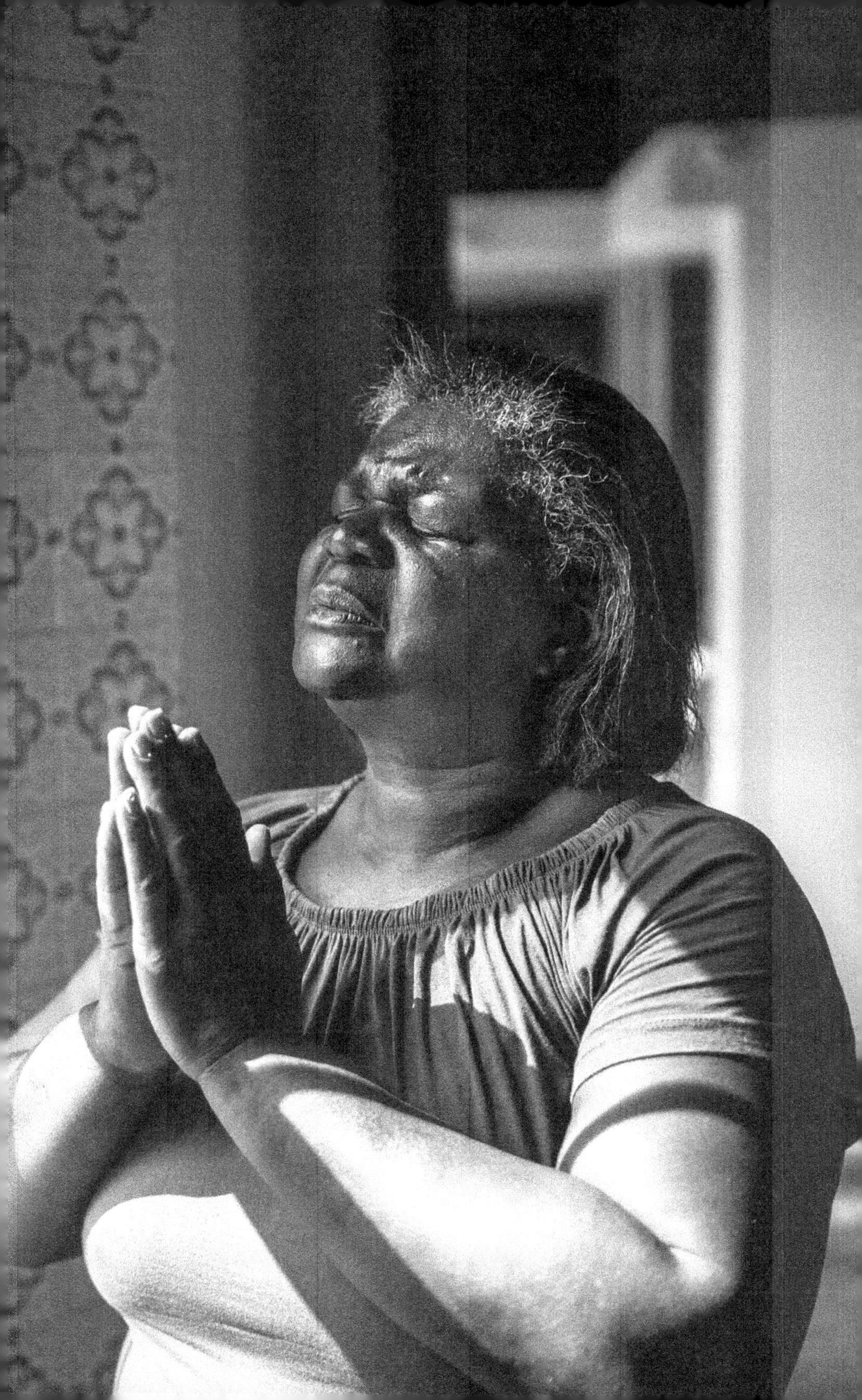

duo, Marjorie Buckman was #1 in everything from the classroom to the lacrosse field, and even the theater room! There was nothing that she could not do.

This exchange was in response to an email Rue received declining her application for an internship. This was the third denial she received. Rue had a set a goal of knowing her summer plans before Margo returned to school for the spring semester. It was not working out the way she planned. She believed she was not accepted because her experiences in high school were not as vast and interesting as her sister's. The spirit of failure was overtaking her.

"I'm pretty sure God just forgot to dump enough magical glitter into my special talents pool when He was up there creating me!" Rue hollered again as she opened her door to further explain her list of reasons about not getting accepted to any of the summer programs.

"Rue, you're literally a senior in HIGH SCHOOL. You have forever to apply for an internship that will impress your future bosses once you graduate college!" Margo explained, as she stood outside of her sister's doorway.

"You don't know that!" Rue responded.

"But I do, Rue. I didn't even work until I got to school. You KNOW this to be fact. Even though I was very involved in high school by playing tons of sports, my body is starting to pay for that," Margo said trying to persuade Rue.

Despite the overwhelming feeling of defeat, Rue decided to listen to her sister for once. She asked Margo to pray with her that she find peace within the closed doors and that she continue to believe that what is for her would be granted to her.

Margo stood up and said, "God always reveals His will for us when we ask Him to. You have to be direct with Him and ask Him to calm your spirit so that you can hear the pureness of His message to you."

"Okay, okay!" Rue said.

"Wipe those tears from your face because as you realign your spirit to a resting state, God can come in and show you opportunities that you couldn't have known existed," Margo said as she wiped away her sister's tears and held her in her arms for a warm embrace.

APPLICATION

What are we supposed to do when we feel that our spirit is no longer aligned with the Lord? You know that feeling when you are the only one walking around in the world with the rain cloud, but everyone else seems to be enjoying rainbows and sunny weather? That type of feeling is only temporary. It typically means we need to retreat to the basics and ask God to make everything still around us so we can remove our fog to only see and hear from Him.

The God we serve is a compassionate one, filled with an overabundance of love and comfort. I think we forget often that everything He does for us is out of love. The next time you are in a season of fear of missing out, ask God, "What is it that you're protecting me from?" rather than "Why can't I have what I want?" Watch the shift that occurs in your life because you have restored your hope in Him and begun to wait patiently for what He has already declared to be yours!

PRAYER

Dear Lord, I pray that You shift my perspective to seek out what You are trying to teach me in moments of solitude and fog instead of becoming upset that I am getting rejected. I know that I should not be concerned with others' success because You have already mapped out my life. I need to trust that what You have in store for my life is greater than anything I could ever imagine. The spirit of rejection and failure, I rebuke. Please fill my spirit with acceptance and encouragement. Continue to order my steps in my life as You see fit. I will wait patiently for You to direct my path! In Jesus' name, I pray, Amen.

DAY 4
WONDERS OF THE HEART

Will He love me?

"*Fear thou not; for I am with thee: be not dismayed; for I am thy God: I will strengthen thee; yea, I will help thee; yea, I will uphold thee with the right hand of my righteousness.*"

(ISAIAH 41:10)

STORY

Bzz Bzz — Voice Memo: *Rueeee! It's me, why do you always have your phone on do not disturb?! I'm having one of my moments and you aren't picking up…*

What the heck?!

It was normal for the sisters to leave each other voice memos during all hours of the day. While it bugged their mom that they used their phones as walkie-talkies, she secretly enjoyed catching them doing it because it reminded her of when they were little and used to carry their pink Barbie walkie-talkies everywhere they went.

"I was actually driving this time Marjorie," Rue tried to convey in a convincing tone to her sister. Meanwhile she had fallen asleep at Aleeya's house up the street.

"What's up? What is this *so-called* emergency you have, girl?"

"I'm experiencing that thing again where my heart is beating out of control. It literally feels like it's going to pump out of my chest!" Margo quickly tried to explain in one breath.

"1-2-3-4-5, breathe!" Rue said as soon as she realized her sister was having her second anxiety attack of the day.

Margo had been having anxiety attacks since before the two became sisters. When they were waiting to be adopted, Margo always shared her fear of never getting to know what it would feel like to have someone love her unconditionally. As a parentless child, she did not know how or if she would ever be able to feel that feeling. Rue was always too young to understand what she meant by that, but always gave her the tightest bear hug whenever Marjorie felt anxious.

"Can you please come home?" Margo asked. "This one isn't slowing down like the regular ones do," she cried through the phone.

Within minutes, Rue was on her way back home. She stayed on the phone as she drove. As soon as she pulled into the driveway, she quickly stepped out of the car and scurried into the house to find Marjorie curled up on the floor in their living room.

Rue scooped her up into her arms and began rocking her gently. She reassured Margo that for as long as she was around, she'd always be there to pick her up and fill her with love. Then she began singing to her their favorite childhood song, *Jesus Loves Me*.

More often than not, Margo felt as if God no longer loved her for all the hurt that she carried around in her heart as a child. She always remembered learning in Sunday school how God wants us to love one another, unconditionally, as He loves us. Yet, how could she forgive and love without bounds her two parents who left her to fend for herself before she could even speak?

Somehow, Rue always knew when Margo needed to hear that song the most. The song immediately brought both to tears because it had carried the two of them through some extremely tough times. They were grateful that through adoption, they had learned how to feel Gods' love.

APPLICATION

It is a scary time in life when we feel that we no longer deserve God's love. Imagine harvesting so much hatred in your heart that you end up punishing yourself so that you never know what peace, joy, and calmness feel like. Being wrapped in God's love is equivalent to always feeling warm and fuzzy inside. He is such a constant in a world made up of indecisive people.

God chooses us daily. That knowledge alone should be enough to allow you to release any hate in your heart that is preventing you from forming a pure relationship with God. He makes sure that we are always able to have the love we need whenever we need it. This is another testament to His selfless love. Being able to feel God's compassion through His divine love is a top tier experience that we should never want to lose!

Prayer

Dear Lord, I want to feel the fullness of Your love for me. Please remove any ounce of hatred or evil spirit within my heart that may be taking up space that belongs to You. Soften my heart so that I can learn to have compassion and love Your people the way that You do—without restrictions. I will no longer hold onto memories and emotions that evoke fear within my spirit. Continue to use me as a vessel to attract more people to Your Word. I ask that You forgive me for harvesting hate, and that You grant me mercy and grace to begin a new journey of love. In Jesus' name, I pray, Amen.

DAY 5
WONDERS OF THE WORLD

Will He hear me?

"For the Lord God is a sun and shield: the Lord will give grace and glory: no good thing will he withhold from them that walk uprightly."

(PSALM 84:11)

STORY

"What's that story again?" Margo asked as she plopped herself onto Rue's bed.

"What story are you talking about, Marjorie?"

"You know, the one you keep telling mom and dad about how you've been talking to your birth parents—which we BOTH KNOW IS FALSE," Margo leaned in and hollered into Rue's ear since she did not take off her headphones to engage in the conversation.

It had been a couple days since the issue arose. Rue had been in contact with her folks, but it was weird? She honestly thought Margo would have dropped it, but she did not. Rue's biological parents had been reaching out to the adoption agency to find where Rue was located. It turned out that they lived only a few towns over from her.

"Girls! It's time to go. If we don't leave now, I'm going to have to sit behind Sister Kim. That means I won't be able to see a doggone thing!" their mother complained out of the passenger seat window.

"We're coming," they shouted running out the front door.

"Ma, I was wondering if we could wait just a little bit longer?" Rue asked. My parents said they'd show up on time today to catch a ride with us," Ruby pleaded with her mom.

"Ruby Arie, get your butt in this car!" her mother said. "We can't keep waiting every week for them to show up and then we're late."

Rue rolled her eyes and replied, "Fine." She gave her dad and Margo a displeased look because they didn't help her plead her case.

For months, Rue had been prompting her biological parents

to go to church with her. During the alter call on Sundays, she took Margo down for prayer with her and asked the deacons to pray the same prayer every week. All she wanted was for them to recommit their lives back to the Lord and not the world. Rue's parents came around every so often, but they were always under the influence of drugs or alcohol. In her mind, the environment in which they lived was the cause of their behavior because it did not expose them to a different type of life.

"Hey, look who it is!" Margo whispered to Rue during the sermon.

As she glanced to the back of the church, she saw two figures that appeared to be her parents. Her prayers had become reality. The way the sunlight hit the middle aisle where they were entering made it feel surreal, almost like the scene out a movie! The tears began to fall from Rue's eyes, and naturally Margo's too.

"I knew they'd make it; it's their time," Rue said as she leaned over to tell her parents. Then she met her biological parents in the aisle with her arms spread wide open to hold them both.

Application

How do we know that we aren't praying in vain? It's simple. God tells us to cast all of our worries and fears onto Him so that we do not have to carry any burdens of our own. Sometimes, it is going to feel as if all we are doing is praying, and we aren't receiving the things we desire.

When this happens, we have to thank God for all of the blessings that He is pouring into our lives that we cannot see. We have to thank Him for waking us up. We have to thank Him for nature and its ability to function without man's involvement. These things show us that God is a purposeful and intentional God. Everything He created in this world serves a purpose and will do miraculous things to keep the order.

Prayer

Dear Lord, thank You for not just hearing my prayers, but for showing up and answering them. There are millions and millions of people in the world, but somehow You still carve out time to hear me and my worries and silence all my doubts. I pray that You allow me to bear witness to Your work in the world both on a personal and global scale. Continue to show me Your miracles daily so that I can draw more men unto You. For those who do not believe in Your wonder, send them unbelievable works that can only be described by You. In Jesus' name, I pray, Amen.

FIRE - TERRI L. HANNETT

JANUARY
WEEK 7

DAY 1
PREPARING FOR THE FIRE

Do you know how to identify the fires in your life?

"Why art thou cast down, O my soul? and why art thou disquieted in me? hope thou in God: for I shall yet praise him for the help of his countenance."
(PSALM 42:5)

STORY

Barbara had been feeling a little overwhelmed. She was busy managing her full-time job as a print buyer, taking care of her family—two young children in elementary school and her husband—plus completing online classes to earn her MBA. Despite small bumps in the road, she thought everything was somewhat under control. What she could never have imagined was that her normal pace of juggling life would soon be turned upside down.

Due to the COVID pandemic, her children had to attend school virtually from home, which required adult supervision. In addition, her office closed when several staff members contracted the virus. This meant that she, too, had to work from home. At first, this seemed like a blessing, and she mapped out a plan for her and the children. However, Barbara's husband was laid off unexpectedly from his job. Everything seemed to be going awry.

Barbara had always been very private. Even through this stressful transition, she kept everything bottled up inside, convinced that she could manage the new normal. Unfortunately, the pressure impacted her ability to focus.

APPLICATION

Often, changes and challenges happen so quickly that we do not take the time to stop! Regardless of what is happening, we must slow down to assess our internal response to the outward pressures. When we quiet ourselves, we will be able to see, hear, and think clearly.

God is never surprised. He has an exit plan in place for every season in our lives, but we must be able to hear His instruction and willing to accept the path He wants us to take. There are a few strategies that will help you walk according to God's plan for your life. These include: 1) listing your concerns in a journal; 2) identifying scriptures that speak to each challenge; 3) communicating with a family member, friend, or church leader and; 4) meditating and praying each day.

Reciting the Word of God is also empowering and sheds spiritual light on the journey. Perhaps, the purpose of this season is for you to draw closer to God. Remember, fire is symbolic of testing and purity. God is with you. Pray His will, not your own. Begin to praise the Lord regardless of what is before you. Your victory may be in your immediate future, or you may realize it later in your spiritual journey. Remember that God loves you, and He knows your challenges. God is the author and the finisher of our faith.

PRAYER

Lord, there is so much that I'm dealing with right now. You knew I would be here at this time in my life. Please help me in this season to trust You to guide me. Lord, I depend on You to provide wisdom, guidance, comfort, and strength. I receive Your help, and I will praise You, Lord, through my journey! Let Your will be done, not my will. Thank You, Father, for never leaving me nor forsaking me. Thank You for holding me up when I am weak and giving me the strength to press forward when I can't see what's ahead. You are my strength, and my help comes from You. Lord no matter what happens, I will praise You. In Jesus' name, I pray, Amen.

www.urbanspirit.biz

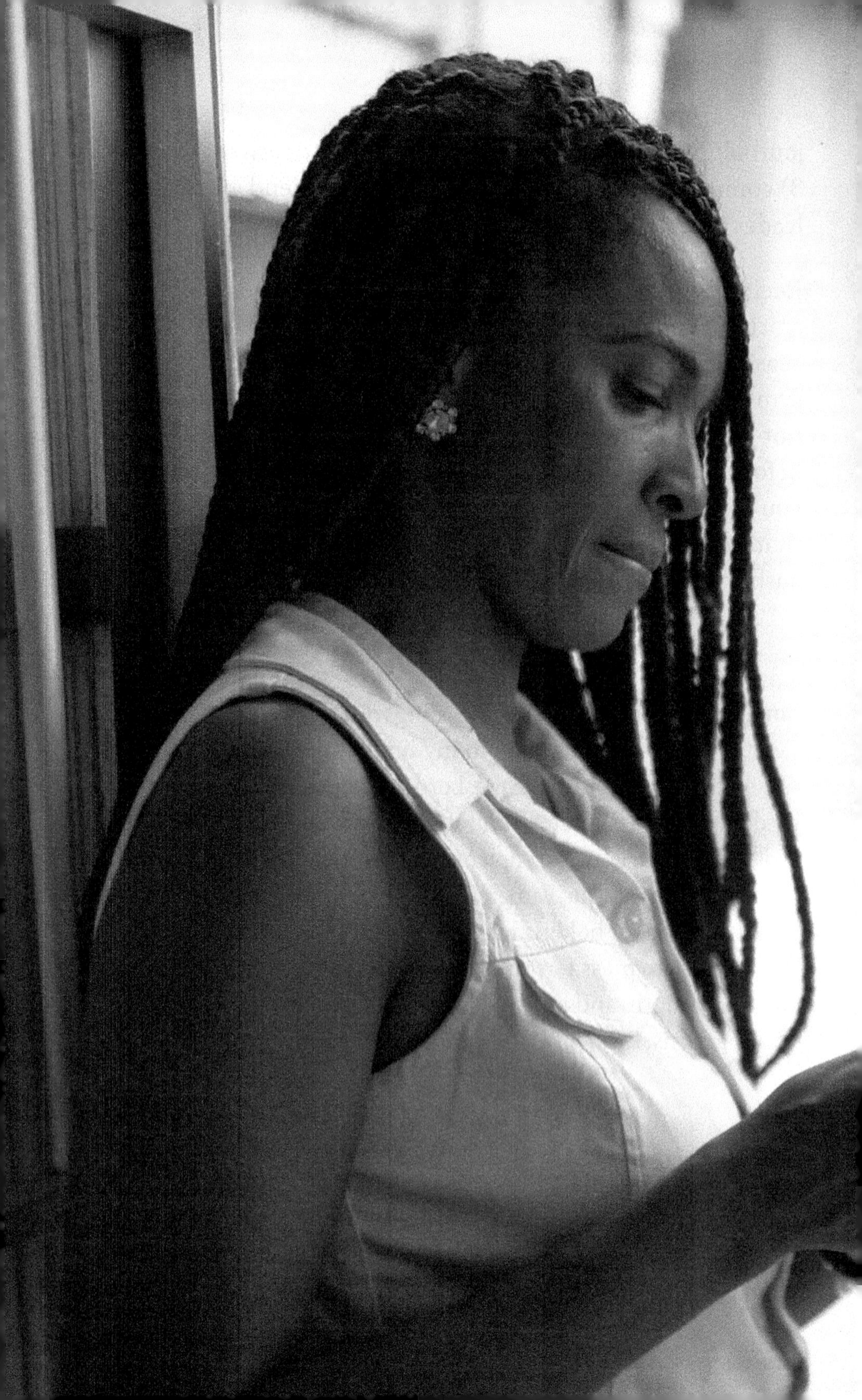

DAY 2
GOING THROUGH THE FIRE

Do you trust God when you can't see Him?

"Trust in the Lord *with all thine heart; and lean not unto thine own understanding. In all thy ways acknowledge him, and he shall direct thy paths."*
(PROVERBS 3:5-6)

STORY

One day, Tonya, Barbara's best friend of thirty years, called.

"I've noticed that you have been a little withdrawn," Tonya comment. "Is everything okay over there?"

Barbara put her best voice forward. "Yes, sis.

We're doing great! I have some systems in place, and we are all good."

Listening closely, Tonya sensed that things were not quite right, so she jumped in her car and drove to Barbara's house to bring school supplies for the children and some spa items for her friend. She was shocked to see her friend's well-appointed home in total disarray when she arrived.

"Barbara, what's going on?" she asked. "Tell me so I can help you."

Barbara collapsed onto the sofa as tears burst from her eyes. "I don't know what happened," she lamented. "It's just too much! I'm on a roller coaster and can't get off. I feel like I'm all by myself. John is too depressed to help. My job is more demanding than ever, and I can't keep up with the children's class schedules or keep them engaged on Zoom every day. Plus, I have two-hour Zoom meetings to attend for work! I don't know what to do! Where is God in all this, Tonya?"

APPLICATION

In the midst of a crisis, it is difficult to remember that the Lord has brought us through challenges in the past. If we look back over our lives, we can see the hand of God. List all of the things the Lord has done for you in the past. His grace and mercy kept you then and will continue to keep you. He will never leave you nor forsake you.

The trials of life reveal the true condition of the heart and the strength of our faith. Consider these steps: 1) acknowledge what you are going through; and 2) create an environment of balance. The Serenity Prayer is a great way to remind yourself that some things might be out of your control. It is important not to suppress your feelings nor keep them bottled inside. Let your friends and family know how you feel. Allow them to assist in whatever ways they can.

Prayer

Heavenly Father, You are my strength. I am grateful for Your written Word, which guides me during difficult times. Thank You for teaching me how to stand and trust You. Thank You, Lord, for grace and mercy. I will praise Your holy name and give You all the honor and glory as You prepare me for what is to come in my life. Lord, remove all fear and remind me that You are with me. Thank You for the strength of the Holy Spirit. I surrender my life to You. Surround me with the right people at the right time. Lord, I give You all the praise and honor. Ignite my faith as I stand on Your written Word. In Jesus' name, I pray, Amen.

DAY 3
FAITH IN THE FIRE

How strong is your faith?

"*For we walk by faith, not by sight.*"
(II CORINTHIANS 5:7)

STORY

When Barbara's boss notified her that her department would be placed on furlough because of supply chain shortages, she did exactly what she had been taught not to do as a believer—she panicked! Her heart began to race, and she was in a frenzy. Her husband had been laid off, and now this. She paced the floor with tears flowing down her face as she questioned God.

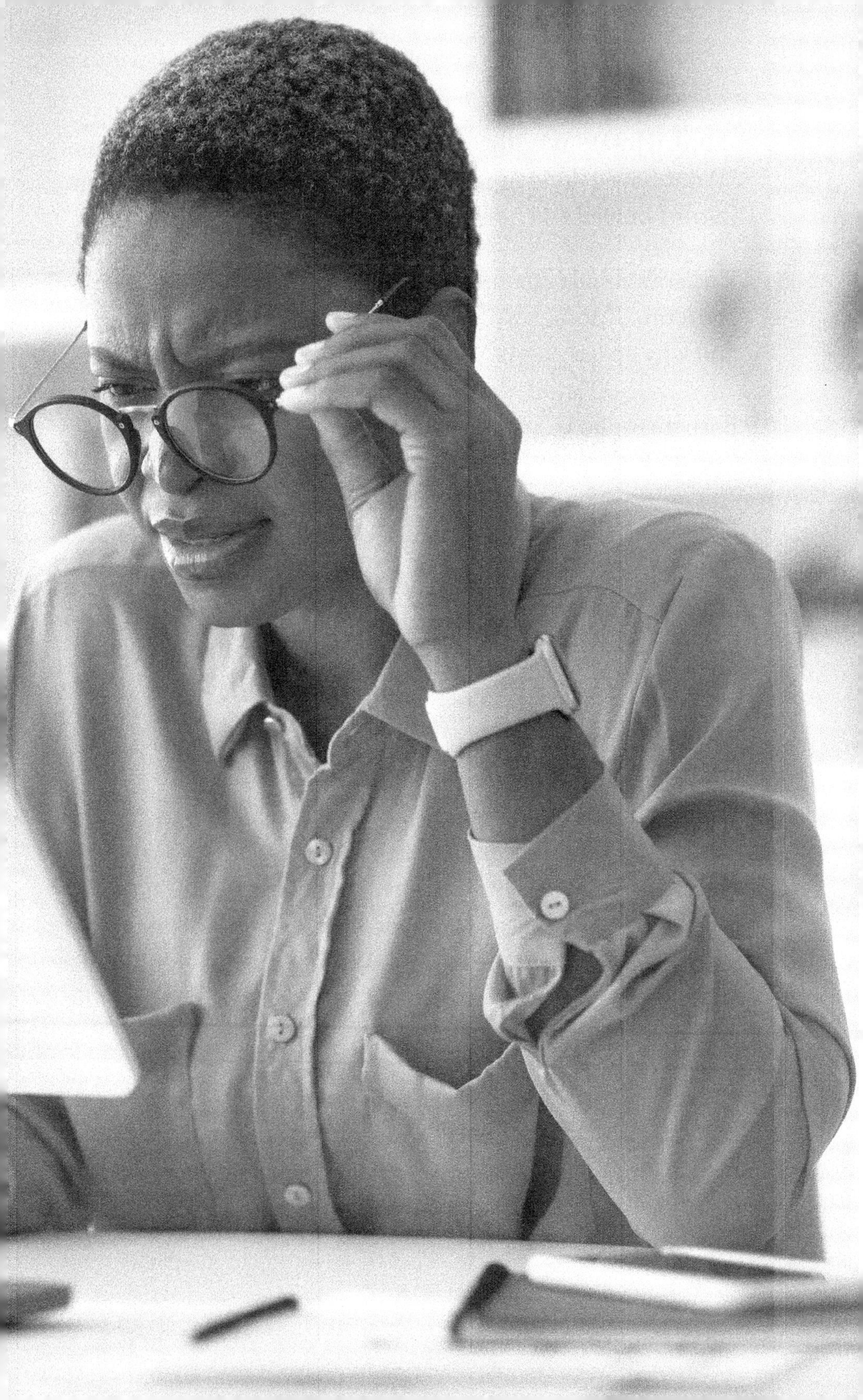

"Lord, why are You allowing this to happen to me?" she asked. "What have I done to cause this? Why are You punishing me, Lord? I prayed and prayed, and I don't know what else to do."

Barbara's youngest son, David, overheard her and came into the bedroom. "Mom, what's wrong?" he asked. "What happened, and why are you crying?"

Barbara replied, "Son, I may not have a job."

"It's going to be okay, Mom," David assured her. "Just like you have always told us, God knows everything and He will never leave us."

Barbara held her son tightly as she dried her tears and thanked him for reminding her that the Lord was with them.

APPLICATION

When we are in a crisis, it is difficult to remember what the Lord has done for us. The Bible teaches us that weeping may endure for a night, but joy comes in the morning. Get up! Go take a walk and pray as you walk, like Jesus did. Worship the Lord and give Him thanks for the ability to move your limbs. Immerse yourself in nature and revel in the presence of the Lord.

Allow the Holy Spirit to speak to your heart to clear your mind of all the clutter and distractions. Find a dedicated time in the morning and during the day to incorporate a breathing exercise. You need to have a method of relaxation that you can employ anywhere. Deep breathing keeps our nervous system regulated during times of stress and anxiety. Quiet your spirit and be intentional. Exhale the problems you are wrestling with and inhale God's peace. Your goal is to regain peace and restore balance. Remember that the trials of your journey draw you closer to Christ.

Remind yourself that God is with you and He cares about your circumstances. It is imperative that you know this and move with a level of confidence. You have direct access and a gateway to communicate with the Lord through prayer. Take all of your problems to Him.

Prayer

Lord, Thank You for Your grace and thank You for Your mercy. There is nothing too hard for You. You are my help in times of trouble. There is no situation too difficult for You and nothing that You will not take care of on my behalf. I ask You to speak to me, Lord, and give me clear insight and clarity about the next steps. Help me not to be anxious about anything as I seek You in prayer. I worship and praise You, Lord, for who You are! You are my protector, my shield, and my help in times of trouble. Thank You, Lord, for sustaining me and upholding me during difficult times. In Jesus' name, I pray, Amen.

www.urbanspirit.biz

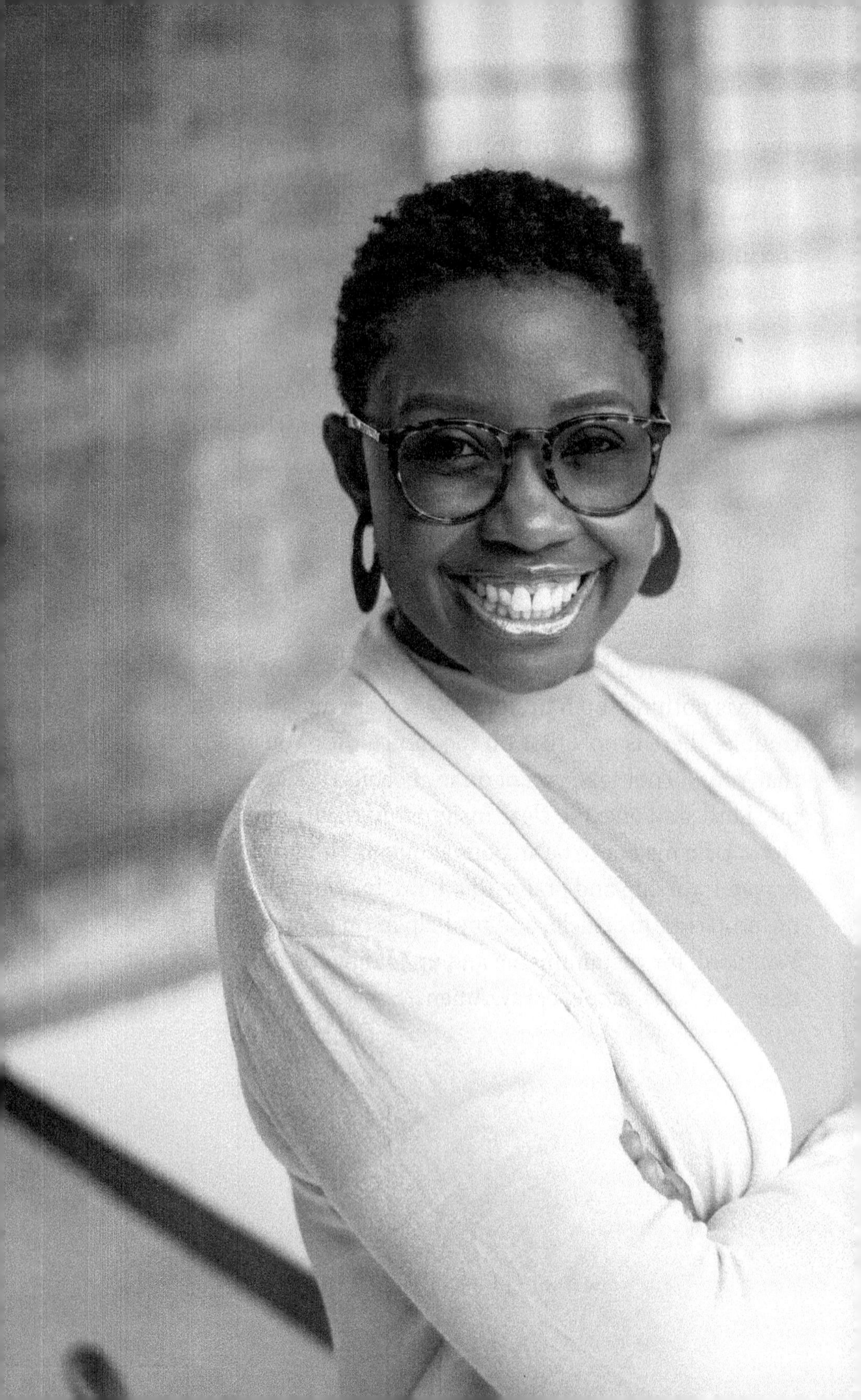

DAY 4
PREPARATION AFTER A FIRE

Do you know how to care for yourself after the fire?

"Wherein ye greatly rejoice, though now for a season, if need be, ye are in heaviness through manifold temptations: That the trial of your faith, being much more precious than of gold that perisheth, though it be tried with fire, might be found unto praise and honour and glory at the appearing of Jesus Christ."
(I PETER 1:6-7)

STORY

For several weeks, Barbara was intentional about changing her mindset related to the challenges she was experiencing. She began reading a daily devotional again and decided to go back to church on a regular basis. While attending the weekly church service, the pastor asked members of the congregation who were struggling with hearing from God to come to the altar for a special prayer. Everyone was encouraged to commit to two weeks of fasting and praying to draw closer to God.

Barbara shared her commitment to fasting and praying with her long-term friend and accountability partner, Tonya, who supported her by joining in the fast. Abstaining from certain foods and other distractions renewed their spirits as they consecrated themselves to God. Peace filled Barbara's heart and she began to feel a sense of balance coming back. She encouraged her husband and helped him search for job opportunities. Tonya found a tutor at the church who would help Barbara's children with their homework and assignments during the week. Barbara was grateful for her friend Tonya, who walked with her through it all.

APPLICATION

As we read the Word of God and meditate day and night, we renew our minds. We think clearer and begin to move and react differently. So often, people shut down by withdrawing from God when life is tough. In difficult times, we should shift gears, lean into God, and draw near to Him!

The Lord does not delight in our pain, sorrow, or disappointments. Everything we experience is for a reason and purpose, even though we may not understand why we must endure various challenges. One day the dots will connect, and our journey will reflect ways the Lord shaped and molded us for His glory.

Valley moments are times to invite others to walk with us. Why not identify someone you trust to fast and pray as well as talk to about your struggles. Be diligent and praise the Lord and He will reveal His plan to you. Remember that your answer might come to you in a different form than what your eyes can see. The Lord desires to shape our hearts and create newness in all of us for His glory.

Prayer

Lord, I am grateful for Your written Word, which never returns void. Throughout the generations, You have proven that You are faithful. Your Word assures me that I am not alone in all that is happening. Thank You for the Holy Spirit's comfort. Lord, I give You all the praise, honor, and glory for bringing me through the fire. Thank You for directing me to pray, wait, and trust only You. Thank You for giving me a faithful prayer partner. Thank You for the blood of Jesus Christ shed for me. Thank You for every mountain You have brought me over and every valley You have seen me through. Hallelujah! In Jesus' name, I pray, Amen.

DAY 5
REFINED FROM THE FIRE

Do you recognize your strength?

"But the God of all grace, who hath called us unto his eternal glory by Christ Jesus, after that ye have suffered a while, make you perfect, stablish, strengthen, settle you."

(I PETER 5:10)

STORY

The spiritual disciplines of prayer and fasting strengthened Barbara. The Holy Ghost empowered her to continue her journey and feel more confident. So that she remembered this experience the next time she went through a challenge, Barbara bought a journal to record her feelings.

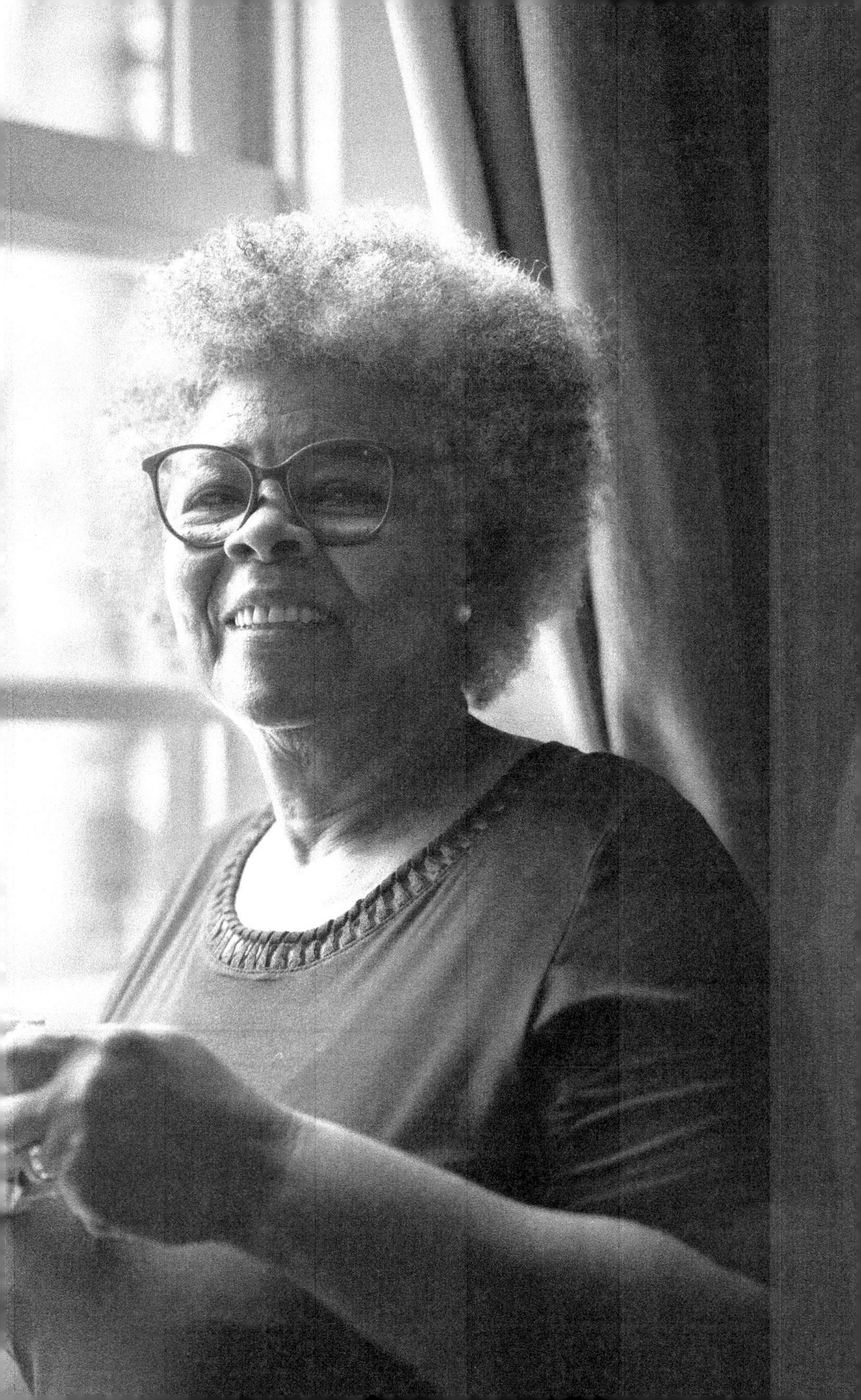

She wrote down her prayers along with the scriptures and inspirational songs that encouraged her.

"Tonya, thank you," Barbara said with tears in her eyes. "You have helped me make it through one of the most difficult times in my life."

"Girl, that's what friends do," Tonya replied. "We've been there for each other for most of our lives. We grow together, learn together, and overcome together. I've got you and I know you've got me."

Barbara was amazed that having an accountability partner strengthened her relationship with God. She was determined to help someone else the same way Tonya helped her. She knew what it felt like to be disappointed, afraid, and overwhelmed, and she would never criticize anyone else for feeling the same way. Instead, she decided to do what Tonya did—be available!

APPLICATION

The trials of life help shape, develop, and identify our spiritual weaknesses. Like the physical strength test that we take at the doctor's office, trials assess our weaknesses and identify areas for improvement. Spending time with God in daily devotion, having an accountability or prayer partner, prayer, fasting, and journaling are spiritual practices that help us grow.

Sharing your feelings and experiences are important parts of your growth and the growth of others. Honestly sharing our feelings with trusted friends and even strangers can help us to remain humble. We do not have to pretend to be spiritual giants! We need one another.

When the difficult times are over and we are on the other side of that test, it is time to celebrate. Rejoice with praise and thanksgiving because God has proven Himself faithful on your behalf. Rejoice because God has brought you through challenges. Rejoice because you are not alone.

Why not tell others what the Lord has done and be the encouragement that discouraged person needs? Our silent tears, fasting and tarrying in prayer, journaling, and agreeing in prayer with others produce a purpose greater than we realize. When we come through the fire, we learn that God truly does give beauty for ashes. May God bless you as you mature in faith and become a light for the Kingdom of God.

Prayer

Lord, I am so grateful that You have Your hands on my life. Thank You for being concerned about me. Thank You for shaping me and molding me to mature in my faith and my relationship with You. Thank You for Your goodness and mercy! Thank You for friends who help me handle the tests and trials of life, Lord. I thank You for the reminders that You are always right there by my side. I love You, Lord! I give You all the praise and honor because You are worthy. You are the author and finisher of my faith! I will worship You forever. In Jesus' name, I pray, Amen.

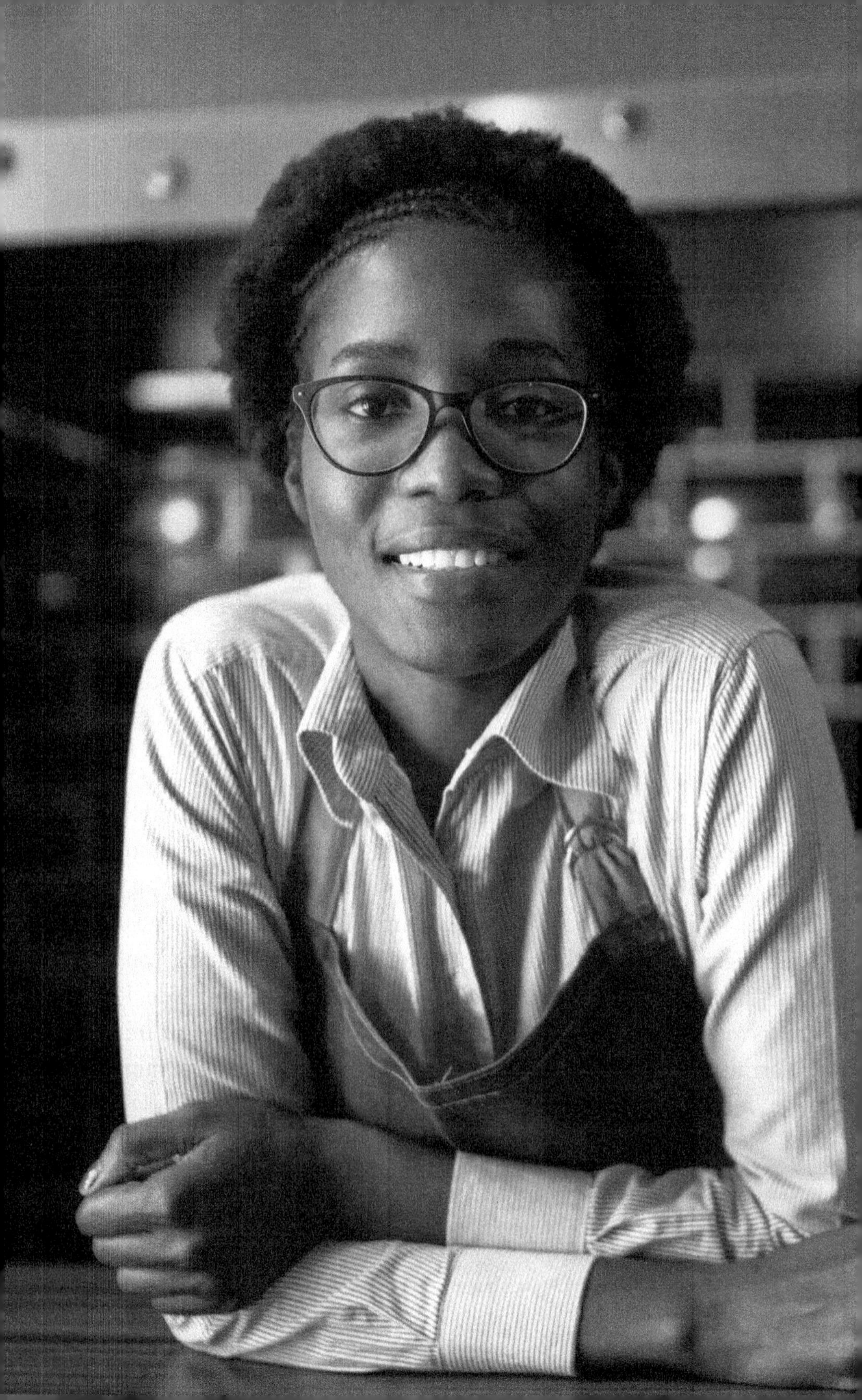

LIGHT – FIRST LADY KELLI JONES

JANUARY
WEEK 8

DAY 1
REVEALING LIGHT

How can you see in darkness?

"For thou wilt light my candle: the Lord *my God will enlighten my darkness."*
(PSALM 18:28)

STORY

In a moment, the lights went out. It was the dead of winter. The days were already short and the nights were long and dark. Anne was in the middle of responding to a work email when she was suddenly engulfed in darkness.

"Mom!!!!! The power went out!" yelled her ten-year-old son.

"Yep, I can *see* that. No pun intended," she replied. Anne knew she had paid the electric bill so the other option was to check the breaker box to see if a fuse had blown.

The fact that she was sitting in the dark was symbolic for how she had been feeling inside. Work was overwhelming. She was having some serious problems communicating with her husband, and her son, though just feet away in the other room, had grown emotionally distant. Darkness, it seemed, was not just her outward reality, but her inward one, too.

Where is that flashlight, she thought to herself. The breaker was in the basement and she knew she would need some light to find her way safely.

APPLICATION

Many of us often feel as if we are engulfed by darkness. When Saul chased after David, he literally ran for his life. He hid in dark caves to escape harm. It is not surprising that David used the imagery of a lamp to describe the deliverance that came from the Lord. The image of light shining in darkness paints the picture of God delivering David.

Darkness causes uncertainty, fear, and stumbling, among other things. When light shines in darkness, it reveals obstacles and a safe path. When we experience the darkness that can come with life, we should ask God for His revealing light in our lives. Only the Lord can bring the revelation needed to illuminate a dark situation. Darkness and light come and go with the

www.urbanspirit.biz

rotation of the Earth, but God is continuous light for us, no matter the circumstance.

Prayer

Father, when darkness closes in around me, help me to remember that I can call on You to light a path for me. Thank You for being my light in this dark world. With Your help, I do not have to sit in darkness indefinitely. I ask for Your light Lord to shine in and through me in times of darkness. Lord help me to remember that I have access to a never-ending source of light. I thank You Lord that You are with me even when I cannot see You through the darkness. Help me to remember, Lord, that Your light drives out darkness. In Jesus' name, I pray, Amen.

www.urbanspirit.biz

DAY 2
BRIGHT LIGHT

Where is the light within you?

*"Thy word is a lamp unto my feet,
and a light unto my path."*
(PSALM 119:105)

Story

Anne slowly and carefully made it to her pantry. The frustration she felt was mounting. This power outage could not have come at a worse time.

"I guess there is no convenient time for sudden darkness," Anne thought out loud. Pulling the pantry door open, she was relieved to locate the bright yellow flashlight almost immediately. With the flashlight in

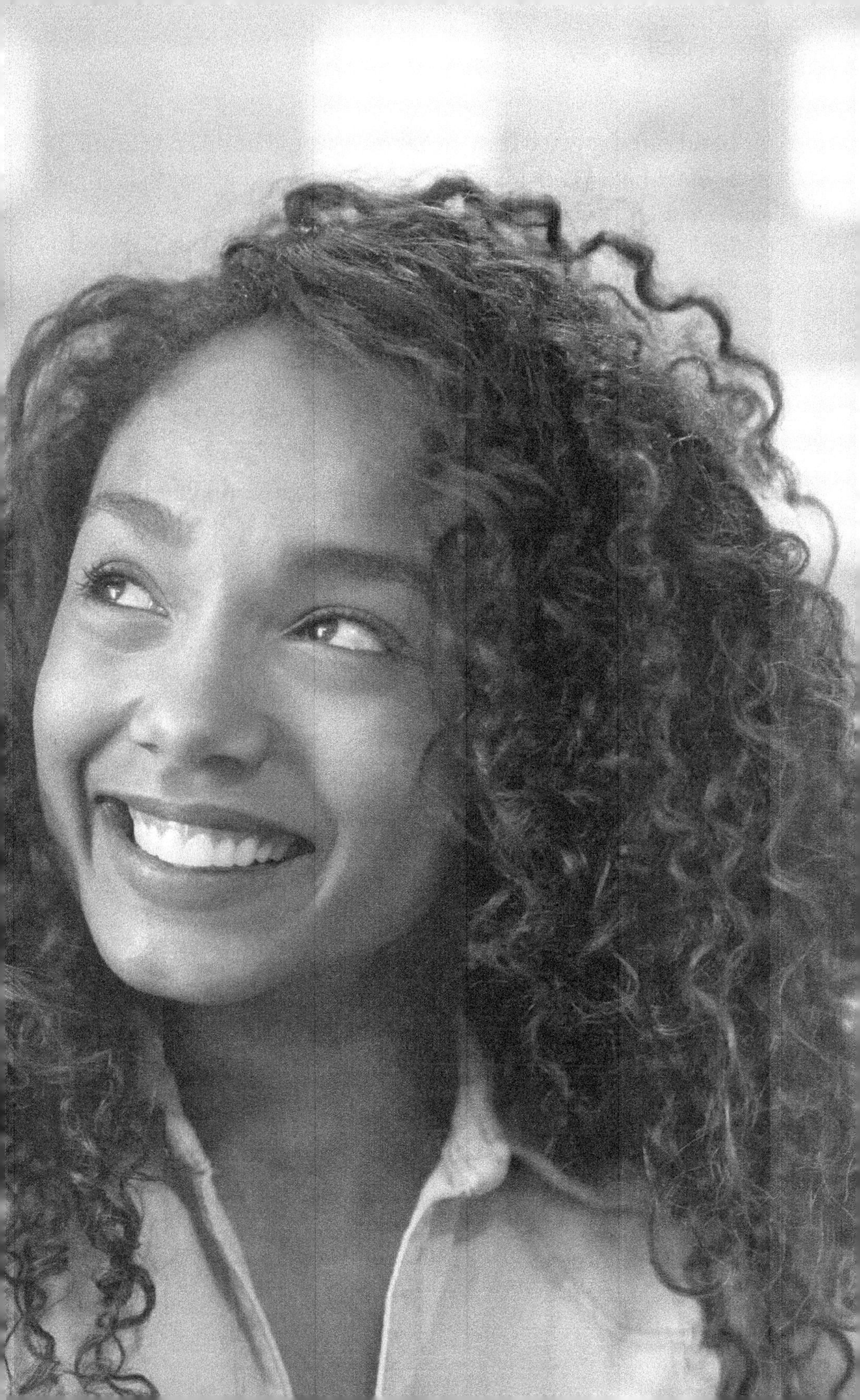

hand, she expected the whole house would be up and running again. She was mistaken.

Click...nothing...Click. There were no batteries in the flashlight. The sigh Anne released was so loud that it actually resulted in a reaction from her son. "What now!?" he whined.

It was just a few more feet to the junk drawer, but it felt much further. Anne was so close to light, yet it seemed to slip from her desperate grasp. When she reached the drawer, she quickly felt around the collection of random items and grabbed two batteries. She popped them in and finally *LIGHT!*

It was amazing how even a little light made such a difference. The stream of light breaking through the darkness gave Anne a new confidence that there was a coming end to the darkness in her life.

APPLICATION

Anyone who has tried to walk in complete darkness can attest to the frustration and fear that accompany such an endeavor. Unlike cats and other nocturnal animals, human eyes are not meant to see well in darkness. We need light. Light allows us to see cracks and obstacles that must be avoided for safety. It is amazing how even just a little light shone in the right direction can keep one from stumbling.

The Bible describes God's Word as a lamp and a light. When uncertainty surrounds us like darkness, we can turn to God's Word to guide us. This does not mean that there will be no obstacles or barriers in our way. It means that the Word of

God can and does provide us with direction as we journey on in life. The light of God's Word may guide us to wait patiently; it may guide us to tell the truth lovingly, or it might guide us to spend more time in prayer with the Lord. The light of God is bright enough to lead us if we follow it.

Prayer

Father, I thank You that You did not leave us on this Earth without guidance. You have given us the light of Your Word to help us live rightly before You. When I am troubled, confused, and unsure, help me to remember to go to Your Word for guidance. Help me to mediate on it day and night and to use it to inform my movements. Help me, Lord, to cling to Your Word like I would to a flashlight in the dark and to shine it before every step that I take. In Jesus' name, I pray, Amen.

DAY 3
DIRECTING LIGHT

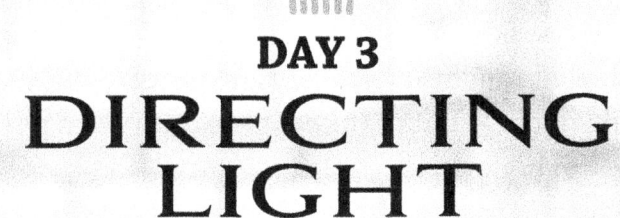

Are you following the right light?

"Then spake Jesus again unto them, saying, I am the light of the world: he that followeth me shall not walk in darkness, but shall have the light of life."

(JOHN 8:12)

STORY

Anne clutched the flashlight with both hands as if it weighed fifty pounds. She had come too far at this point and did not want another setback. Dropping the flashlight might have led to her just giving up and sitting in the darkness. She pointed it down at a slight angle so that she could see five steps ahead of her. She had not realized how many of her son's belongings were on the floor. She stepped over shoes, a helmet, and his bookbag. She thought it was funny how differently you view things when you are forced to look down and examine every step that you take.

As Anne opened the basement door, she felt a new rush of gratefulness for her flashlight. The stairs were steep and the floor at the bottom was concrete. A misstep would be a disaster. Light brought such clarity and peace to this blackout. Anne could not help but to think of the clarity and peace that she needed in her own life.

"I wish I had a spiritual flashlight," Anne sighed as she descended the steps.

APPLICATION

Jesus is the light of the world. As the conductor of our lives, He provides the same type of guidance, comfort, and peace that comes when light floods darkness. The fact that Jesus came to Earth, died for our sins, and was resurrected illuminates any dark situation that we encounter. Jesus secured our eternity with His death, burial, and resurrection. When challenging and dark circumstances are viewed through the lens of salvation, we can count on God to direct and guide our steps.

When we are in darkness and searching for light, we must be careful about the light we choose to follow. We must be sure to follow the light of the Lord. His light will lead us in the right direction and on the path that He has prepared for us. Other lights will lead us astray. It is important to know the difference between God's light and the world's light. If you follow His light, you will never walk in darkness.

Prayer

Thank You, Father, for Jesus. Thank You for sending Him to Earth where He died for our sins. He experienced everything that we experience as humans. Help me to remember that Jesus' sacrifice provides a directing and loving light to my life. When I am tempted and feel hopeless in dark times, remind me that I follow the light of the world. Remind me that the light of the world knows me and loves me. Remind me to shine that light on others and on my circumstances. In Jesus' name, I pray, Amen.

DAY 4
WARM LIGHT

Are you letting your light shine?

"Let your light so shine before men, that they may see your good works, and glorify your Father which is in heaven."
(MATTHEW 5:16)

STORY

Anne made her way to the breaker box easily, thanks to her flashlight. A few quick switch clicks and the house was completely flooded with light.

"Yeeeeeeeees!!!!!!" Anne heard her son exclaim. She chuckled to herself as she thought about how something so simple as light is missed so much when it is gone.

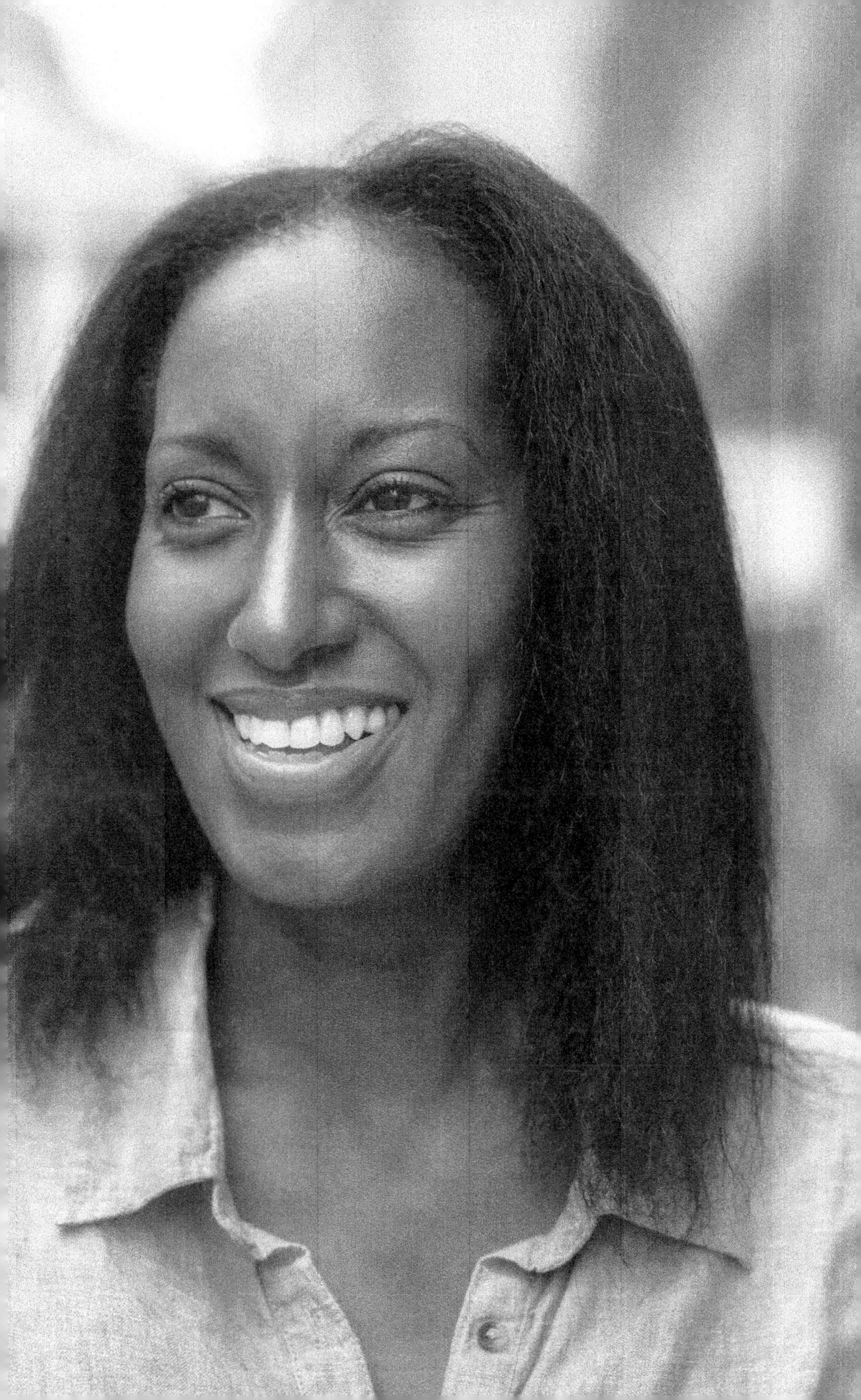

Anne quickly made her way up the stairs and out of the basement. She was met with a hug so sudden that it startled her. "Thanks, Mom!" her son said in a muffled voice as he had buried his face in her side.

"You're welcome, sweetie," she replied.

Her son had been distant and grouchy and Anne appreciated this sudden display of affection. If all it took was flicking a few breakers to get this type of reaction from her son, she might schedule weekly power outages.

Anne realized in that moment that just as restoring light to the house brought joy, God sending Jesus as the light of the world had brought her an eternal joy. The blackout served as a reminder that though life could be dark, she had access to the ultimate light that could never be extinguished.

APPLICATION

Light is wonderful when we have it in our lives, so why would we keep it to ourselves? When we have the opportunity to share light with others, we become vessels that share God's love. When we are loving, giving, and serving others, we serve as light in the world. Light reveals characteristics that you cannot see in the dark. Some light even provides warmth, such as the light that comes from a fire.

Jesus was not just content to come to Earth, live, and die. He served and blessed others everywhere He went. His fame spread because of His good works. Jesus did not hide or keep all of the blessings for just His inner circle. He shared openly and readily to those who were willing to receive it. As we follow the glowing example of Jesus, so too should we shine our light openly by our kind deeds toward others. Jesus shares His light so that we can turn around and share it with others.

PRAYER

Father, thank You for Your warming light that You shared with us when You sent Jesus. May Jesus' example encourage me to share that same light with other people. Help me to give, serve, love, and forgive others out of a thankful heart. Lord, let my kind deeds not point others to me. Let my kind deeds point others to You, Lord. I ask that You allow me opportunities to shine Your light on others to draw them closer to You. Thank You for Your light and the opportunity to share it. In Jesus' name, I pray, Amen.

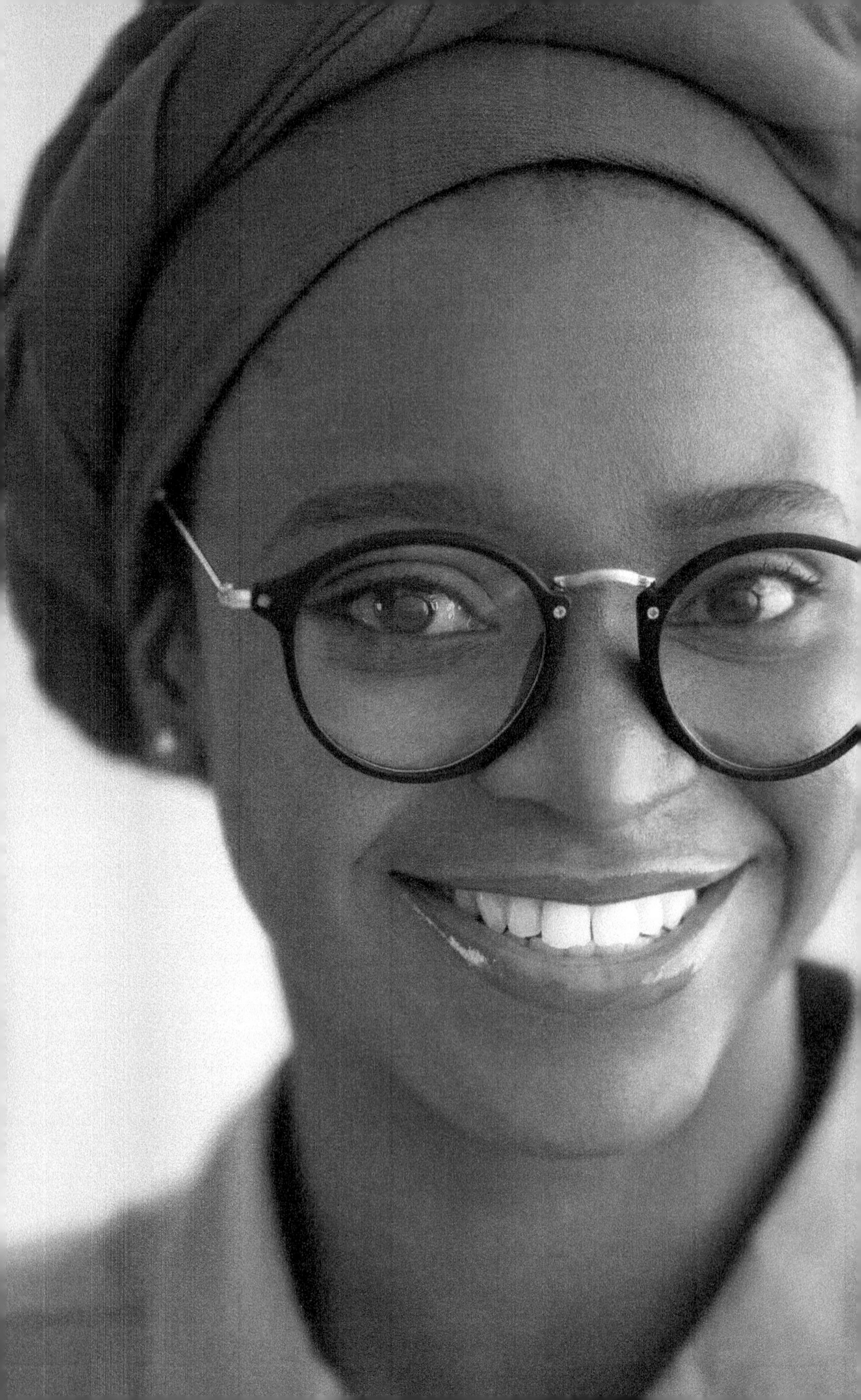

DAY 5
INTENSE LIGHT

How bright is your light?

"And the light shineth in darkness; and the darkness comprehended it not."
(JOHN 1:5)

STORY

Sitting back in her couch with her laptop, Anne realized that the entire ordeal had only lasted about ten minutes. She found it funny how darkness seems to amplify whatever it covers. Anne was reminded of how frustrated she felt when the darkness first fell. She remembered her relief when she found the flashlight and her exasperation when she realized that the batteries were dead. The memory of the joy and relief she felt as the flashlight with new batteries shot a beam of light across the room brought a smile to her face.

Next, she reflected on how, with the guiding beam of the flashlight, she was able to safely traverse the stairs into the basement and fully restore light to the entire home. Finally, the sensation of her son's embrace flooded her heart and mind.

"Light, just the presence of light brought so much joy," she said aloud.

Anne could not help but to think about Jesus and how His finished work on the cross was as guiding, warm, and comforting as that artificial light. Actually, Anne had come to realize that when you have the inner light of Christ, no power outage can ever diminish it.

Application

It is very difficult to create a space of darkness in a room full of light. On the other hand, even a small match instantaneously creates a halo of light in a dark room. Wherever that tiny flame goes in a room, its light pushes away the darkness.

The Bible often describes Jesus and the Word of God as light. This world can be dark, but we should serve as examples of our Savior and the Word of God to help guide us through it. When we encounter darkness, we can turn to the Bible using the guiding light of Jesus' example to navigate darkness.

PRAYER

Father, thank You for the light of Your Word and the light of Jesus. Thank You, Lord, that we do not have to fumble around in the dark. Help me to rest in the warmth and guidance of Your light. Thank You that Your light overpowers darkness. Darkness cannot stand in the face of Your Word. Help me to follow Your light and trust it to lead me in Your ways. In Jesus' name, I pray, Amen.

GO – SHANTEL MOORE

JANUARY
WEEK 9

DAY 1
GO WITH FORGIVENESS

Can you forgive everyone?

"He that covereth a transgression seeketh love; but he that repeateth a matter separateth very friends."
(PROVERBS 17:9)

STORY

Tiffany and Diane had been friends for years. They had their good times and their bad times. Overall, they knew they could share anything with each other and keep it in strict confidence.

One day, to Tiffany's surprise, she overheard Diane sharing something personal about her

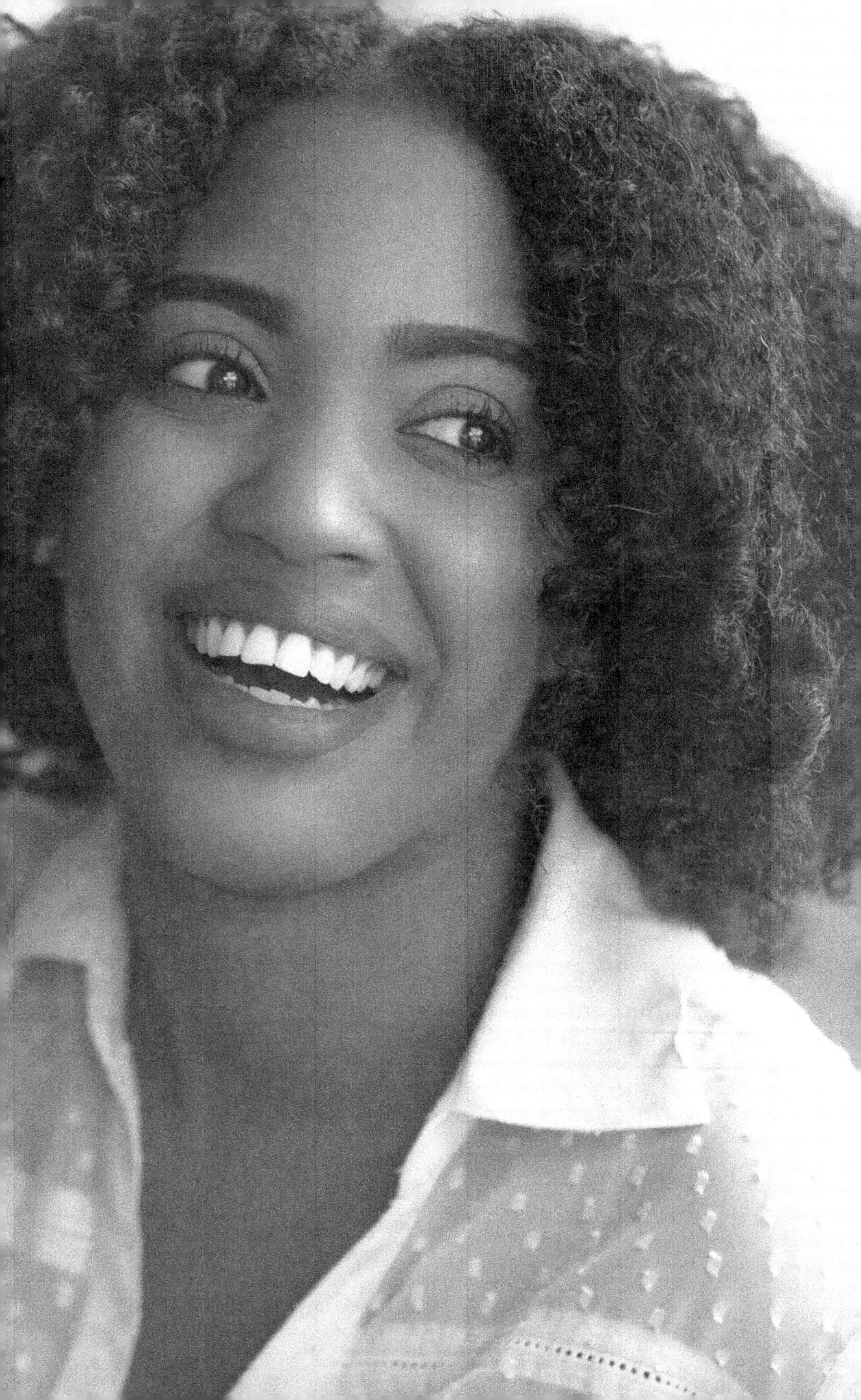

with a mutual friend. Tiffany was hurt. She could not believe what Diane had done. She questioned whether she should forgive her or even talk to her again. Tiffany decided to pray about it. After all, she knew she could talk to God about anything.

In her time of prayer, God reminded Tiffany that unforgiveness is not His way of handling things. God is always quick to forgive when we sincerely repent and ask for it. She decided that she would reach out to Diane to talk.

"Diane," Tiffany said softly. "We need to talk."

"What's up?" her friend asked.

"I heard you tell Lisa about something that I shared only with you," she said disappointedly.

After a brief silence, Tiffany said, "I am so sorry, Diane. Lisa was going through something similar and I thought sharing your situation would be helpful. I realize that I should not have done that without your permission. Please forgive me."

Tiffany felt compassion for Diane, remembering that she is not perfect either. She forgave Diane on the spot, and their friendship continued to grow.

APPLICATION

Forgiveness is God's way of keeping our hearts clean before Him. We should never want to hold onto unforgiveness because it breeds strife, anger, bitterness, and resentment. Forgiveness, on the other hand, breeds love, understanding and unity. In life, we will all have to make the decision of whether we should forgive someone. We could justify why we shouldn't forgive, but God's Word is clear. He freely forgives us when we ask with genuine repentance, and He commands that we do the same for others.

Think about a time when you had to forgive someone. How did God use that experience to show His forgiveness toward you? How does it feel when you hold on to unforgiveness? Do you feel free, or do you feel bound to the person who you have not forgiven? When you walk in unforgiveness, you are holding on to the pain and reliving it over and over again. I once heard it said that unforgiveness is like drinking acid and thinking it will hurt the other person. God wants you to walk in total freedom. That freedom comes through continually forgiving those who hurt you.

Prayer

Dear Lord, it's not easy to forgive people who hurt me. I don't want to hold onto pain because I know that keeps me far from them, and ultimately spiritually distant from You. Help me to be quick to forgive and to remember that You are always ready to forgive me, even when I do not deserve it. In Jesus' name I pray, Amen.

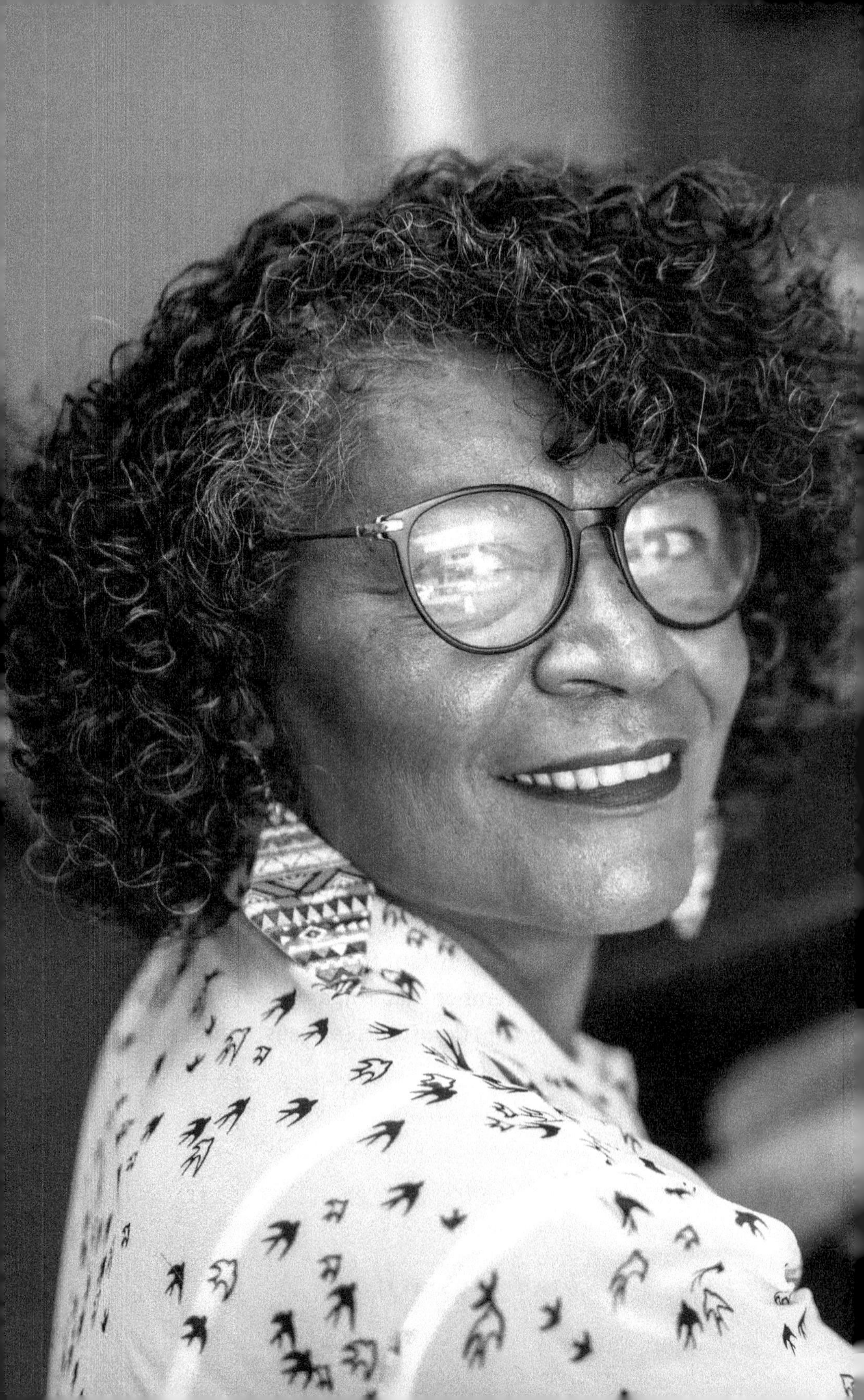

DAY 2
GO WITH LOVE

Can you love everyone?

"But I say unto you, Love your enemies, bless them that curse you, do good to them that hate you, and pray for them which despitefully use you, and persecute you."

(MATTHEW 5:44)

STORY

For the most part, all of Tiffany's neighbors were nice people, except Chris. He never spoke when she waved, and he went out of his way to not make eye contact with anyone. Chris was also very rude. Sometimes he would block Tiffany's parking spot on purpose. Chris played loud music late into the night and ignored his neighbors' complaints. His yard was unkempt and he left nasty notes in Tiffany's mailbox when her Life Group members parked on the street.

One night when closing in prayer, her Life Group decided to pray for Chris. His behavior was hard to ignore, and they knew his actions were a result of him not having a relationship with the Lord. Not many days after they prayed, Tiffany decided to take some freshly baked cookies over to Chris. In the box of cookies, she included a kind note saying she was praying for him. She didn't know if her gesture would change anything, but she was willing to try. She even prayed over the cookies before leaving them on his front porch.

A week went by and Chris had not responded to the gesture. However, his front yard was clean, and the loud music had stopped. He even made eye contact and gave Tiffany a half smile when pulling out of his driveway.

"Girl," Tiffany said excitedly when she called Lisa. "My neighbor actually looked at me today. Can you believe it?"

"Of course, I can," Lisa replied. "God answers prayers! Chris doesn't know what came over him."

They both laughed. Tiffany believed that because of their prayers, God had softened her neighbor's heart.

Application

As believers, we are God's ambassadors. We are His representatives on the Earth. God loves everyone, and He wants to use us to love them as well. Just a kind word or gesture could be the very thing that God uses to heal someone from loneliness, depression, or fear. Be sensitive to the Holy Spirit. Ask Him to show you who needs a touch from Him. When a thought comes to your mind to say an encouraging word, write a note, or help a stranger, go with it! You never know what people are experiencing. Often times, their actions are a result of how they are feeling inside.

How can you reach those who are hard to love? Ask God to show you creative ways to share His love to those who may seem unlovable.

PRAYER

Dear Lord, please give me a heart to love everyone. Show me creative ways to guide people to You. Give me Your heart. You died for everyone, not just for the nice people. Help me to see past the negative actions of others to meet their real needs. I am available Lord. Send me. In Jesus' name I pray, Amen.

DAY 3
GO WITH EXPECTANCY

Can you expect God's best?

"Hope deferred maketh the heart sick: but when the desire cometh, it is a tree of life."

(PROVERBS 13:12)

STORY

Tiffany had always been a hard worker. Every job that she'd had since college had been rewarding. However, lately she had been feeling like her career was going nowhere. She knew that God had a purpose for her life, but she didn't know if it had anything to do with her current job.

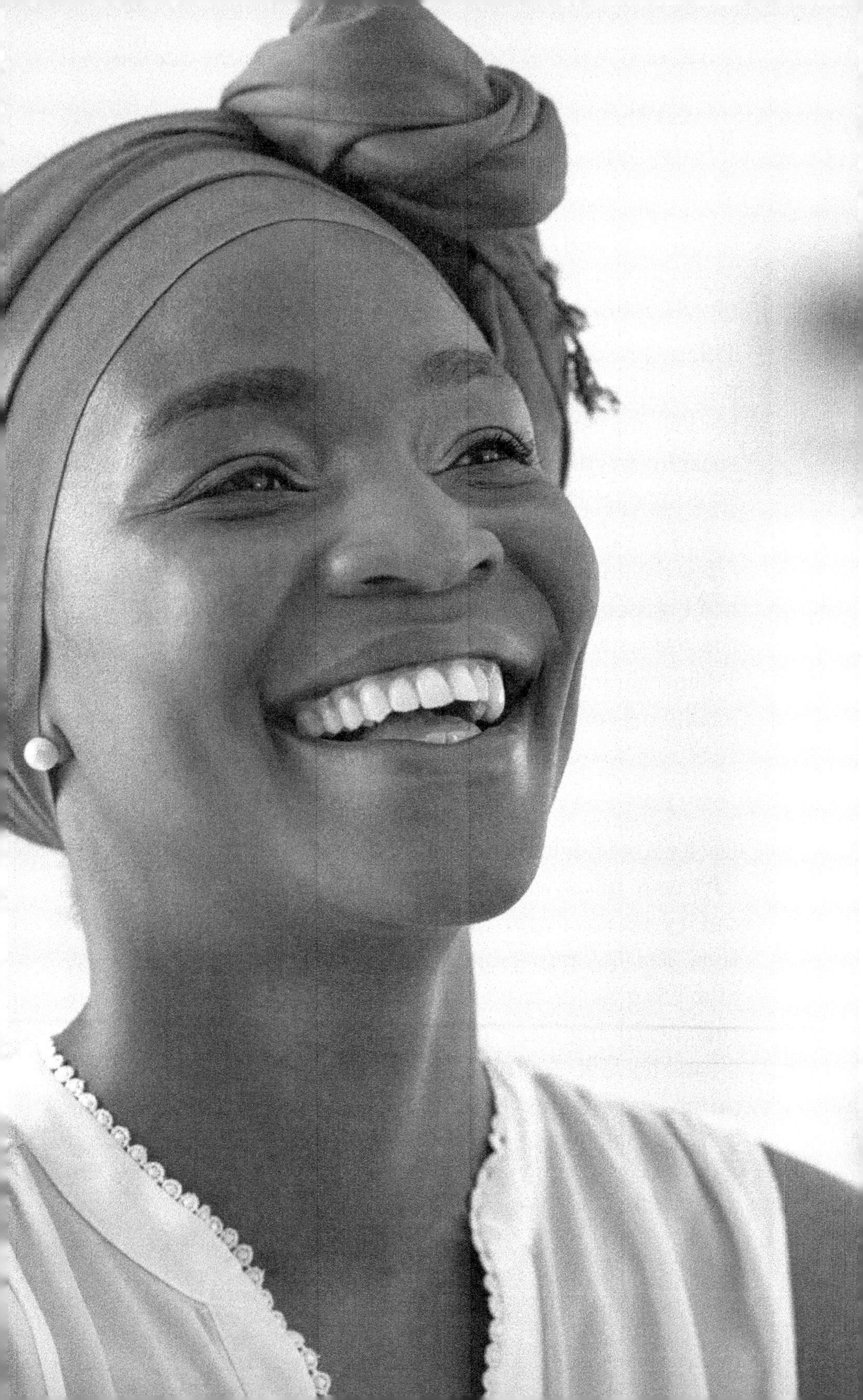

"I feel stuck," Tiffany said to Lisa. "This job isn't fulfilling. I'm like a hamster on a wheel, moving but not going anywhere."

"Take it to God," Lisa replied. "He will reveal to you exactly what you should be doing with your life in this season."

Tiffany knew that she could take her concerns to the Lord in prayer. After praying, she wrote down the things that brought her joy. She listed her passions. Her list included training and speaking to groups. Through this, she felt led to apply for a few training opportunities within her company.

A few days after applying, Tiffany received an email from the training department. They were looking for someone within the company who could be promoted to a training position. Tiffany was interviewed and received the job. She thanked God for the new opportunity.

APPLICATION

Have you ever felt like your life was going nowhere or like your days were full of work, but with no purpose? Sometimes God can use this feeling to prompt you to move toward your next level. The uncomfortable, stagnant feeling could be God's way of making you unsatisfied with where you are or what you are currently doing. That does not mean that you should just pack up and leave your current job or situation. As you pray for His purpose to manifest in your life, He will gently guide you step by step if you yield to His leading.

GO WITH EXPECTANCY

The doors that God opens cannot be closed by man. The only person who can keep God's plan from happening in your life is you. He's waiting on you to ask, seek, and knock. God answers in three ways. Yes, no, and wait. If you step out in faith and the answer is yes, move forward. If you step out and the answer is no, ask for God's redirection. If you step out and the answer is wait, keep believing. In the meantime, sharpen your skills and keep talking to God. He will guide the way. He truly does order the steps of His children.

PRAYER

Dear Lord, I am feeling unfulfilled in my work. All I want is Your will for my life. Please put opportunities before me that line up with Your purpose for my life. I trust You with my future. I know Your plans for me are good and not evil. They are designed to bring me a future and hope. Thank You for knowing what's best for me. In Jesus' name I pray, Amen.

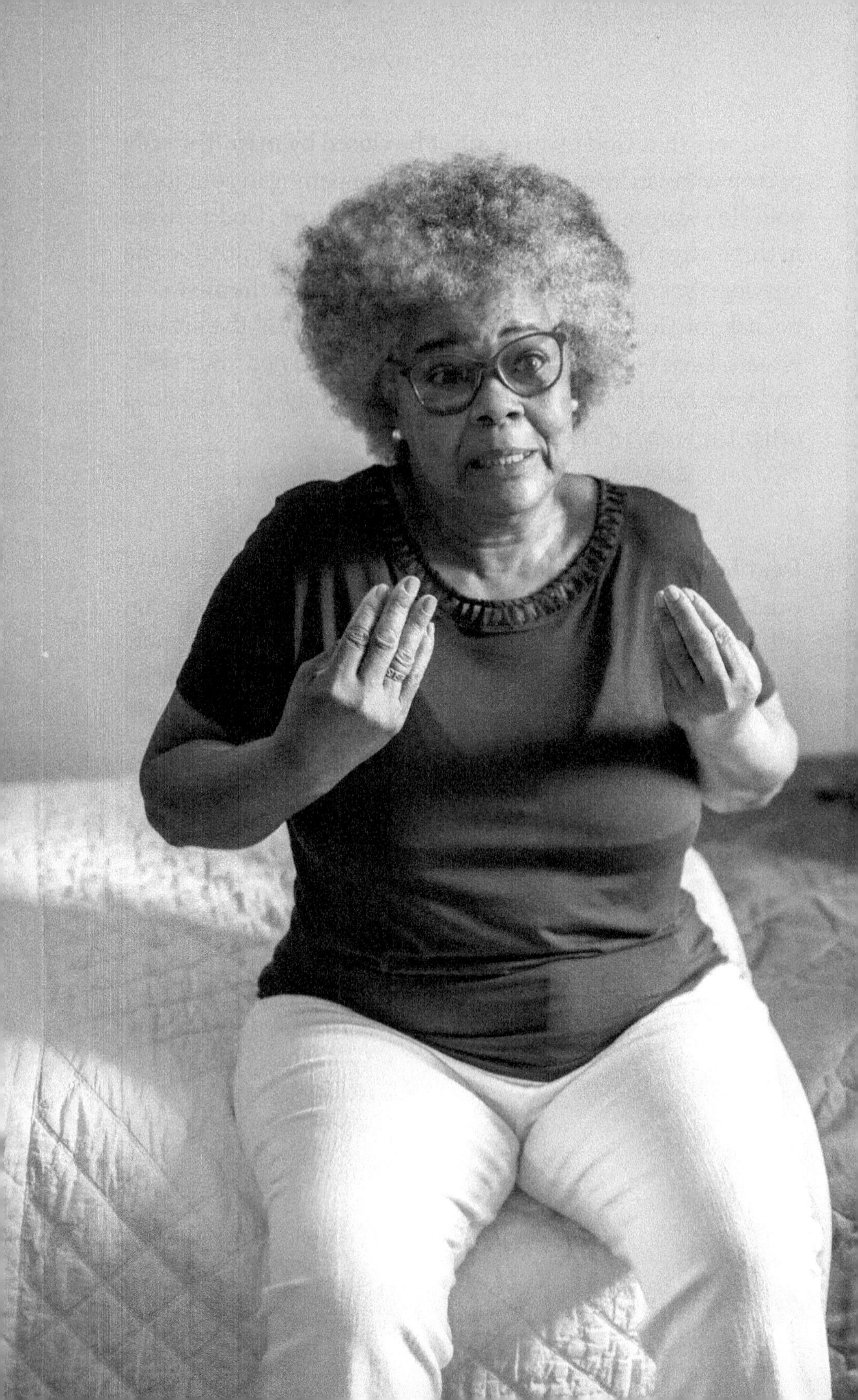

DAY 4
GO WITH GRACE

Can you accept God's help?

"But the God of all grace, who hath called us unto his eternal glory by Christ Jesus, after that ye have suffered a while, make you perfect, stablish, strengthen, settle you."
(I PETER 5:10)

STORY

Tiffany had been in her new position as staff trainer for three months when she started to feel the pressure. It was an exciting opportunity, but stressful at the same time. She was finally working in an area that she felt passionate, but she had a lot to learn.

The expectations were high, and the deadlines were short. Tiffany had come highly recommended and felt like she needed to know all of the answers. She started to wonder if she would meet the company's expectations. What if she didn't measure up? Tiffany knew she couldn't do this without God's help, so she prayed.

Not long after praying, Tiffany was given an administrative assistant, Sheila. Sheila had been in the training department for years so she could be a great asset to Tiffany. All Tiffany had to do was ask for her help. It would take humility for her to tap into Sheila's wisdom, but Tiffany believed that God had sent Sheila as an answer to her prayers.

"Sheila, I need some help with this," Tiffany admitted after spending too much time trying to figure out how to set up one of the company's training modules.
"I thought you would never ask," Sheila responded. "I'm here to assist any way I can."

Sheila was able to provide valuable information about all aspects of Tiffany's new job. She even shared with her the strategies that trainers applied to meet company goals. Tiffany received the help that she needed and Sheila felt appreciated.

Application

God often puts us in situations that require us to need His help. He knows that when we are weak, He is strong. All we have to do is ask. Then we will receive the assistance that He provides. God is faithful to send us who and what we need.

Sometimes we have to humble ourselves to receive it. Humility doesn't always feel good. Humility means not thinking that you are better than other people because of your race, social class, title, or position in life. God can use anyone.

Remember, God is at work in every situation. Everything is not all about us. His plans include others, and His plans are far greater than our own. Trust that God knows best and accept the help that He sends your way.

Prayer

Dear Lord, I confess that I don't know it all. You know exactly what I need in every situation. Help me to yield to Your ways and plans for my life. Send the right people, Lord. Help me to remain humble enough to recognize the help that You send. In Jesus' name I pray, Amen.

LISTEN – C. DENISE HENDRICKS

FEBRUARY
WEEK 10

DAY 1
LISTEN TO FIND PURPOSE

*How do I trust the voice
I hear inside of my head?*

*"So then faith cometh by hearing,
and hearing by the word of God."*
(ROMANS 10:17)

STORY

Anne seemed to have it all, a thriving career, supportive family and friends, as well as a loving and caring husband. She was even active in her community and church, but she was not happy. In her heart, she longed for more but did not know what that

more could be. She felt empty inside and desired more meaning and purpose in her career, but she did not know how to achieve that.

Being a woman of faith, she knew prayer was the answer. However, she felt that her passionate and, oftentimes, desperate pleas to the Lord were going unheard. When Anne believed the Lord was leading her one way, if an obstacle appeared, she would take another route. On that route, more problems cropped up, causing her to become confused, angry, and impatient. In instances such as this, Anne reached out to her spiritual advisor.

"Suzanne, I believe I've done all I can to discover my purpose... prayer, fasting, books...nothing seems to be working," Anne said in a defeated voice.

"Anne, you are more focused on the doing than the listening," Suzanne responded. "You're a box checker—making lists, completing tasks, but never really sitting still to hear how God wants to lead you. Get in a still quiet place and pray for God to open your spiritual ears. Listen to how your heart responds to the prompts in your mind and truly believe that it will come to pass."

APPLICATION

Anne believed that pleading with God would cause Him to reveal her purpose. She did not realize that the actual journey of life would lead her to her purpose. Oftentimes, the voice we hear deep inside of us, that nudging, is indeed leading us in the right direction. We tend to listen more to our human thoughts and not allow those "God thoughts" to dominate the spaces in our minds. God's thoughts about us are bigger and better than we can imagine. In order to turn His thoughts into action, we must believe and have enough faith in Him to achieve that which He has planned for our lives.

Once we read the Word of God, meditate on it and believe it, we need to trust that the voice inside of us is God leading us on the path to our purpose.

Prayer

God, help me to believe that when I am in a state of peace, reverence, and openness to hear Your voice and not my own, I can yield greater results in all areas of my life as I journey to fulfill my purpose and glorify You in that process. I realize that my purpose is tied infinitely to what You want to see manifested in my life for Your glory. I ask You to lead and guide me so that I walk in Your purpose for my life daily. In Jesus' name, I pray, Amen.

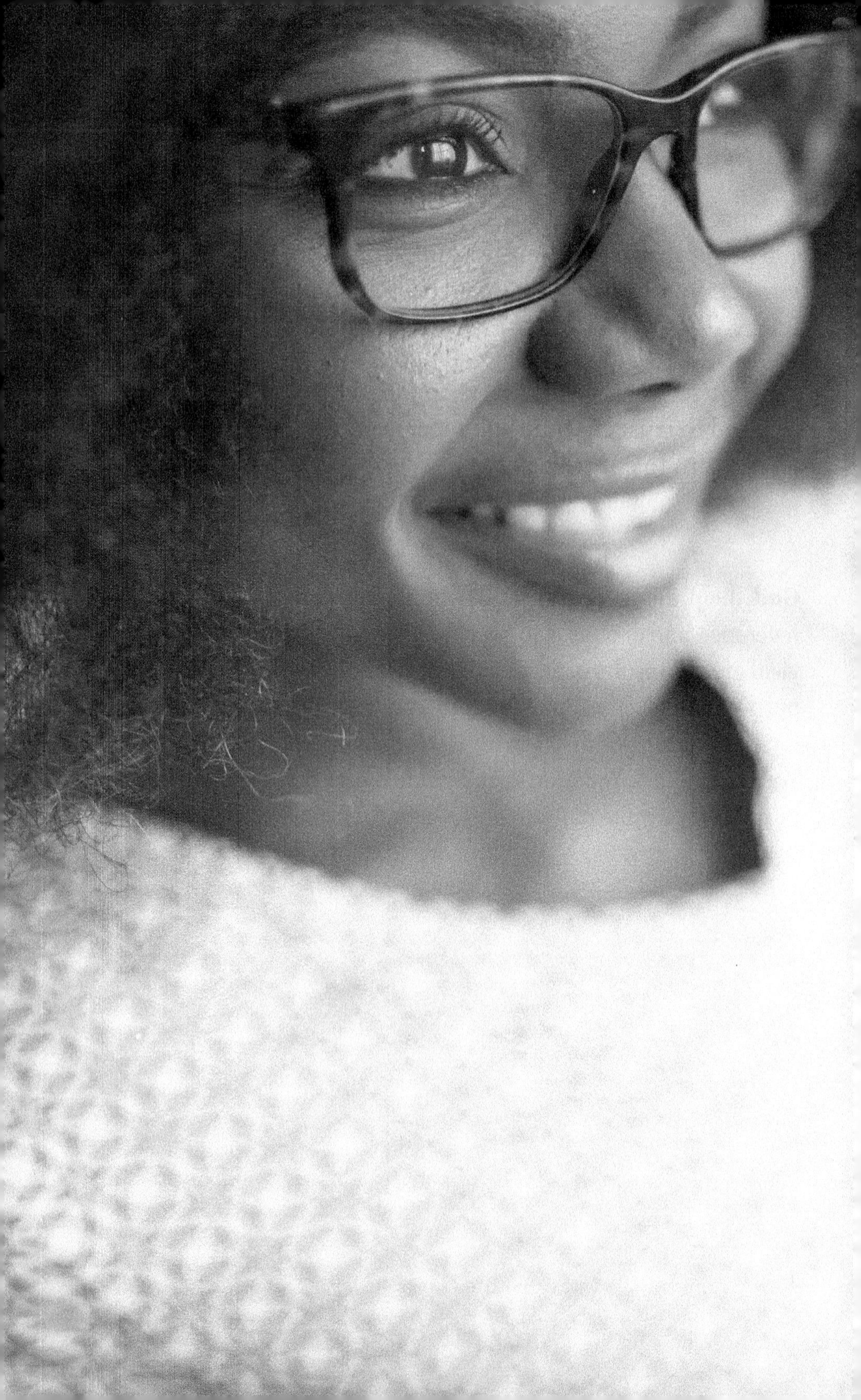

DAY 2
LISTEN TO FIND PATIENCE

How do I hear God when I am too impatient to listen?

"That ye might walk worthy of the Lord unto all pleasing, being fruitful in every good work, and increasing in the knowledge of God; Strengthened with all might, according to his glorious power, unto all patience and longsuffering with joyfulness"
(COLOSSIANS 1:10-11)

STORY

Motherhood was not what Anne expected it to be. She and her husband, Gregory, had battled years of infertility. After a long journey of praying, fasting, and seeking expertise from a bevy of specialists, she conceived at the age of forty-four and gave birth to a beautiful baby girl she named Faith.

At every stage of Faith's life, there were highs and lows, but Anne was always thankful for the gift of motherhood. She just never imagined it would be so challenging, or physically and mentally demanding. Scrolling through social media had Anne believing that parenting was a piece of cake, when it was actually harder than her day-to-day job as a college president.

Faith was entering her teen years and had increasingly become more moody, angry, and defiant. She was fiercely independent and wanted to forge her own path, oftentimes bucking advice and discipline from her parents. Faith's behavior was wearing thin on her parents, especially Anne who found herself constantly arguing with her daughter over low grades, the clothes she chose to wear, and her circle of friends. Faith also told her parents she was done with church and would no longer be attending.

Anne was frustrated and losing patience as she waited for some kind of turnaround. She was too embarrassed to ask for help. They were a successful, upper middle class family that did all the right things, belonged to all the right organizations, attended church regularly, and lived in a neighborhood where their daughter could attend one of the top public schools in the state. Anne had recently shared some of her problems with an old trusted friend, who also happened to be a school counselor and a mother of four.

"Joy, I know we've talked about some of the struggles my husband and I have had with Faith," Anne said. "Now I feel like we are drifting further and further apart from her and will lose her if we don't do something now."

"Anne, good parenting is one of the great mysteries of the world," Joy responded in a comforting tone. "However, I believe you all have laid a solid foundation for Faith and you have to believe and have patience that she will come back around. Stay engaged with her, listen to her, and talk to her, even if she won't talk back. Ask your community of believers to pray for a breakthrough for your family. I think you should also consider family counseling. If you can convince her to go for a set number of sessions, it may yield some surprisingly positive results. Don't give up."

APPLICATION

One of the hardest things for parents to do is to witness their child traveling down what they think is the wrong path. Anne questioned everything she and her husband had done as parents, but could not pinpoint when or why things took a dark turn. However, she realized that by sharing her experiences with trusted counsel, and possibly seeking other counsel, they did not have to go through the situation alone.

God puts people on this Earth to help us through the challenges of life. He does not intend for any of us to do this alone. Ask God to give you a spirit of discernment about the people you should allow in your life to help you through a crisis whether it is through counseling, therapy, prayer, or just plain old good advice. Never be afraid to ask for godly wisdom. Ask God to give you a spirit of patience while you are in the midst of working through any challenging situation.

Prayer

Dear God, I confess I want everything to be alright all the time. When challenges do arise in my life, I want them to be fixed immediately. I know that this is not always possible, but what I do know and believe is that You are the God of turning impossible situations into situations with miraculous outcomes. So today, I pray that You will give me discernment for wise counsel, patience to make it through the storm, and joy knowing that this too shall pass. In Jesus' name, I pray, Amen.

DAY 3
LISTEN TO FIND POWER

How can God's power reveal itself in my life?

"But, when he was in Rome, he sought me out very diligently, and found me."
(II TIMOTHY 1:17)

STORY

Anne found herself embroiled in a scandal she knew was not of her own making. The Board of Trustees at the university she led had accused of her of using funds earmarked for one department to settle a lawsuit from a recently fired employee who had worked in another department. She knew that she would never direct anyone in the finance department to make such a reckless move and wondered how she would get to the bottom of it.

Meanwhile, the accusations and constant questioning of her leadership competency made her feel powerless and overwhelmed. In the three years that she had been at the university, alumni giving was up exponentially, student enrollment was up significantly, and the university had a newly established multi-million dollar endowment. The stress was taking a toll on her mental and physical health. Everyone around her noticed, but it was most evident to her husband, Gregory.

"Anne, it's been a month since the Board of Trustees accused you of wrongdoing with no evidence," he said. You've somehow managed to forget all of your accomplishments and the work you still plan to do for the university. You have allowed these false narratives to weaken your mental and physical health; our home life is a mess, and most importantly, your relationship with God."

"I know Gregory," Anne responded. "This entire fiasco has thrown me off my game. I've neglected my morning devotional and prayer time, and I've allowed others to get in my head. I'm questioning myself and my long record of leading with boldness, integrity, and grace."

"I am here for you, Anne, but only you can pull yourself out of this rut," Gregory responded. "You have to surrender this situation to God and listen for Him to direct your next steps."

APPLICATION

Anne found herself in a situation so embarrassing and debilitating that she spiraled into a level of depression that seemingly knocked her off track. We can all relate. Whether it be with our work life, our relationships, our children, our health, or our finances, there are situations that can literally blind us into thinking there is no way out.

As Christians, we have to remember that there is always a way out. When we learn to totally surrender our situations to God, we can regain that power and operate with the authority and the confidence He gives us to carry out His will. Although it may be difficult, do not succumb to the picture that the world paints of you. Remain grounded in the knowledge that you are a masterpiece created by God.

PRAYER

God, Your Word says You would not put more on us than we can bear, so I know that this temporary setback will only make me stronger. Your Word says You have given us a spirit of power, love, and a sound mind and I receive it in the name of Jesus and move ahead knowing that You have given me the authority and the power to win the race set before me no matter what distractions, falsehoods, or attacks come my way. I can do all things through Christ who strengthens me, and what someone else meant for evil, I know You God, meant it for good. In Jesus' name, I pray, Amen.

DAY 4
LISTEN TO FIND POSITIONING

How do I position myself to hear from God?

"Then Mordecai commanded to answer Esther, Think not with thyself that thou shalt escape in the king's house, more than all the Jews. For if thou altogether holdest thy peace at this time, then shall there enlargement and deliverance arise to the Jews from another place; but thou and thy father's house shall be destroyed: and who knoweth whether thou art come to the kingdom for such a time as this?"
(ESTHER 4:13-14)

STORY

Anne's daughter Faith had only been out of college for three years and was already in her dream job at a tech company.

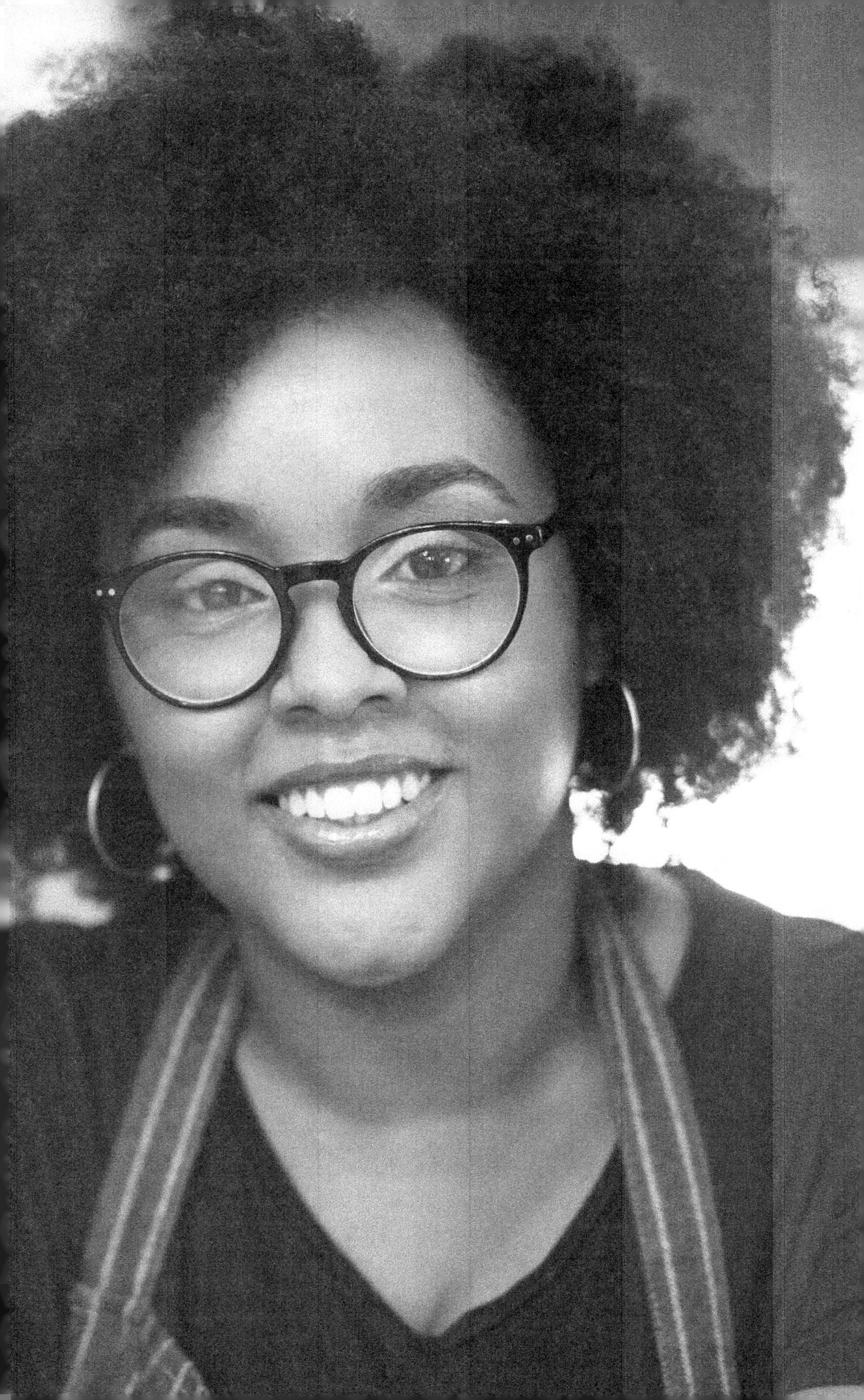

She was thriving in her position and caught the attention of several company leaders who wanted her to take on more responsibility. In a short period, she was promoted and began managing her own team. The new role brought its own unique set of challenges, as she was managing a mostly male team. Many members of the team were significantly older than Faith. There was more travel involved with the new position and the workload had picked up significantly too.

Faith knew she could get it done, but she wondered if the stress was worth it. She questioned why God would put her in this position and give her this much responsibility at such a young age. There was one young man on her team, Michael, who was giving her a particularly hard time. He was frequently late to meetings, openly questioned her decisions, as well as interrupted and talked over her. When she assigned him specific tasks, he refused to do them and asked that they be reassigned to junior team members. His negative attitude and blatant disrespect was taking a toll on her and on morale of the team. She knew she had to confront him or the situation would continue to worsen. This was her first managerial role and she honestly didn't even know where to begin with what she knew would be a difficult conversation. She called up someone she looked up to and often reached out to for advice.

"Hey Dad, how's it going?" Faith asked.

"Hey, baby girl, how are you?" Gregory responded. "How are things going with that promotion?"

"That's actually why I called," Faith shared. "I still love what

I'm doing, but managing people is a lot more difficult than I thought it would be. I think I've taken on too much and I'm starting to question everything I do. I feel like I'm being tested."

"Well, tests are good," Gregory responded. "They make us stronger and better. I don't believe God would have put you in this role if He didn't think you could handle it. Like most people, you are operating on the premise that you alone can solve issues with the team. Allow God to work through you to handle the situation and, in turn, He will get the glory."

APPLICATION

Like Faith, God often thrusts us into positions that sound exciting at first, but once we really get into them, we want to run away. Position can mean anything, not just a job. It could be your position in a new marriage, parenthood, school, church, the community, and other aspects of life.

When you are unsure about a situation, talk to God about it. We could all use some quiet, intimate time alone with God. When we spend time with Him, He will reveal the bigger mission and His will for our lives. The issues that we experience are not always about our personal feelings. Sometimes they are about God helping others through us. Always be willing to allow God to use you, even when it means being placed in uncomfortable situations.

Prayer

God, when You bless me with a position of great responsibility, teach me how to be still and listen for Your direction and guidance. Help to me to block out the naysayers, the haters, and the negative voices that cloud my mind. Help me to consistently seek Your face in all that I do, no matter how big or small the task may seem. Send me sound, Holy Spirit-filled advisers to assist me on this journey. I commit the work of my hands to You. Use me, Lord, as You desire. In Jesus' name, I pray, Amen.

DAY 5
LISTEN TO FIND PEACE

How do I know that God is speaking peace into my life?

"I will hear what God the LORD will speak: for he will speak peace unto his people, and to his saints: but let them not turn again to folly."

(PSALM 85:8)

STORY

After one year of marriage, Faith decided that she wanted a divorce from her husband Craig. She began dissecting every aspect of their courtship, engagement, and marriage. They dated briefly in college, but went their separate ways after graduation, lost contact and had not seen each another in a few years. They reconnected at a homecoming football game, had a whirlwind engagement, and a mostly blissful first year of marriage.

As they entered the second year, Faith found herself embroiled in intense arguments with Craig over everything from money, sex, and even their church life. He became more despondent and spent less and less time at home. They mutually agreed to separate. Now at every turn, Faith, blamed herself for not noticing the signs and wondering what she could have done to keep things together. She couldn't sleep; she gained weight; she stopped going to church and she was missing important deadlines at work.

Faith's parents had been married for close to thirty years. She wondered how she could be going down this path when she had the ultimate example of a loving couple in her parents. She gave her Mom a call to get some answers.

"Hi Mom," she said solemnly. "I have to tell you something."
"Yes baby, what's wrong?" Anne asked.

"Craig and I have agreed to separate," she explained. "I'm not really sure where things went wrong, but we definitely need some space to sort things out and see if we can get back on track. I'm sad, angry, depressed, confused, and frankly embarrassed to be going through."

"Faith, have you prayed about it? Have you all sought counseling?" her mom asked.

"No and no," Faith responded.

"Well, I am not going to tell you to hang in there and work it out," Anne advised. Only you and Craig can figure those things out for yourselves. You also do not need to worry about what others might say, people talk about you when you are happy or suffering. What I will tell you is that marriage is not easy. As you know, and your dad and I have had our challenges over the years. We even separated for a short time when you were very young, too young to remember. I believe what has kept us together is the love and reverence we both share for the Lord and seeing Him work miracles in our lives. We both realize we are not perfect and never will be, but our belief and trust in what God can do has brought us both understanding and peace in our individual and collective lives."

Application

Faith's feelings of despair and shame are normal and valid for anyone going through the dissolution of any type of relationship, especially a marriage. When making difficult decisions, we have to rely on God for instruction, which means we must be in a position to hear from Him. Sometimes, when we go through situations, you drift away from God. Part of the struggle becomes rebuilding a truly genuine relationship with God. Only then can you hear His voice and direction clearly. Only then can you know which way to go.

The Word of God says we can have peace that surpasses all understanding if we bring all of our concerns, our anxious thoughts, and our fears to Him. No situation is too difficult for God to handle. Take everything to Him in prayer. Allow

Him to heal your hurt and give you the strength you need to move past any

Prayer

God, speak peace over my life; speak peace over my mind; speak peace over every situation that has caused me so much pain. Open my spiritual eyes to see and spiritual ears to hear how I can still glorify You. Lord, I want You to have a sense of peace and comfort in the midst of any situation that comes my way in life. Teach me to depend solely on You. In Jesus' name, I pray, Amen.

INCREASE – FIRST LADY JAMELL MEEKS

FEBRUARY
WEEK 11

DAY 1
FAITH INCREASE

Do you have enough faith?

"And he said unto her, Daughter, thy faith hath made thee whole; go in peace, and be whole of thy plague."

(MARK 5:34)

STORY

Ja'nay was so happy. After months of going from doctor to doctor, she finally had a diagnosis. Every doctor she had seen gave her a different diagnosis. She was tired of the needles, the tests, and the medication. She couldn't wait to call her mom.

"Hi Mom!" she said excitedly.

"Hi, baby," her mom responded. "What's going on? You seem really excited."

"I am," Ja'nay responded. "Mom, today I met a doctor who told me he understood what has been happening with my body. After a conversation with him and two tests, he told me that I have a hormone intolerance. The best news is that it can be corrected without surgery! Mom, I have received my increase!"

"That's so good to hear," her mother beamed. "You increased your faith in God, and He answered your prayers. God is good!"

"All the time," Ja'nay replied. "All the time."

APPLICATION

The Bible tells the story of a woman who had been sick for twelve years. She had lost hope and did not believe she would ever be healed. When she heard Jesus was coming through town, she sought after him. She tried one more time! We can learn from her example that increase comes through struggle.

The woman in this story battled all of the obstacles that would deny her healing. She had to battle societal norms that restricted her from going to Jesus. She had to battle the obstacle of the crowds. Because she was considered unclean, no one wanted to be around her. She had to battle to get past the disciples who were protecting Jesus.

Church people sometimes attempt to keep us from Jesus. They put obstacles in our way. They say that we must act a certain way or dress a certain way. They have rules and policies that put a barrier between God and us. When we want something from God, like a blessing or a healing, we have to push past the obstacles. We have to increase our faith and believe in the miraculous power of God.

PRAYER

Father God, I thank You for Your mercy and grace in my life. Father, in You I put my trust. Help me, Lord, to increase my faith. Expand my belief. I want to walk by faith and not by sight. Teach me, Lord, to ignore the voices of the naysayers and to listen only to You. I thank You in advance for my increase in faith. In Jesus' name, I pray, Amen.

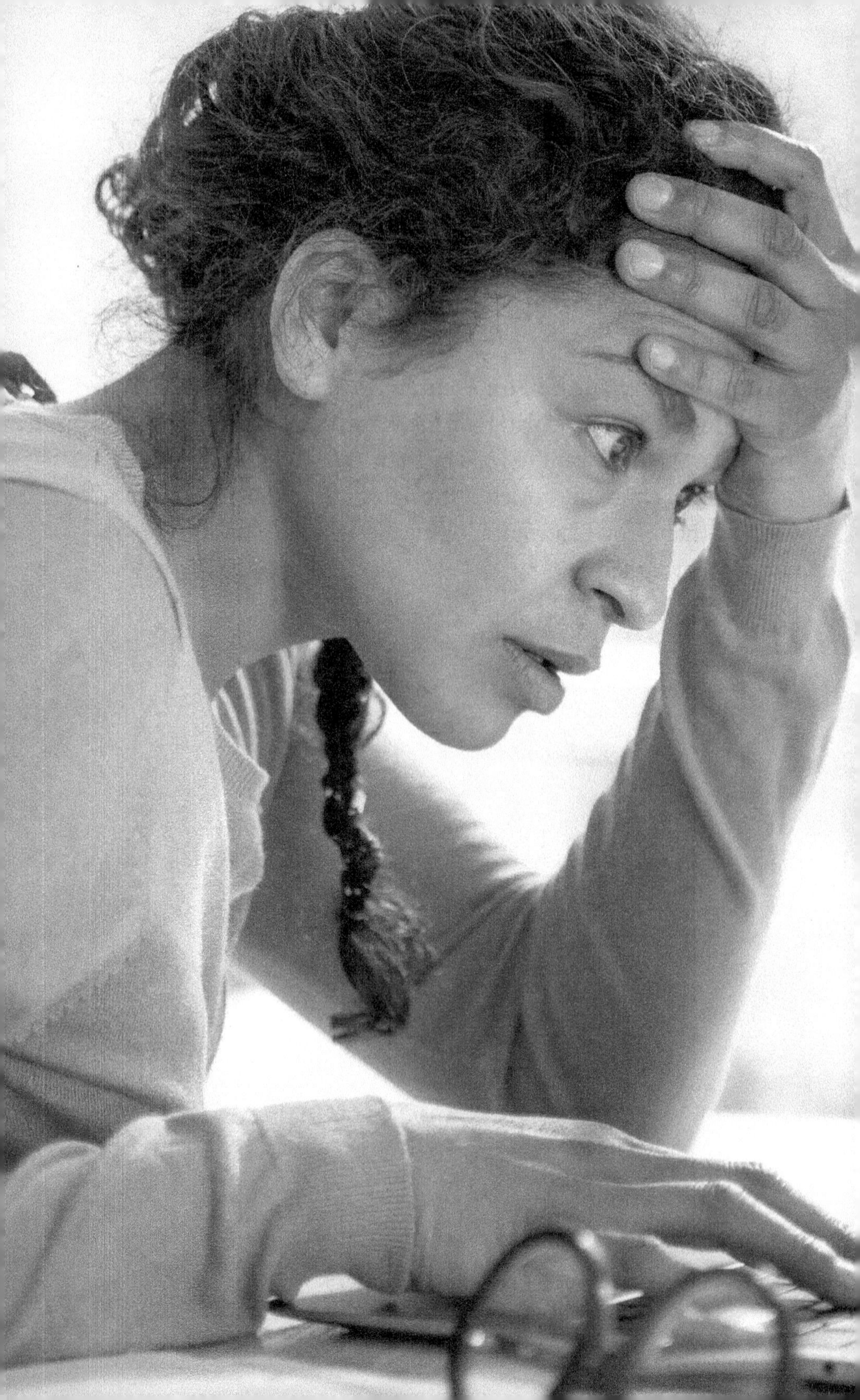

DAY 2
POSSIBILITY INCREASE

Is God the source of your strength?

"Through faith also Sara herself received strength to conceive seed and was delivered of a child when she was past age, because she judged him faithful who had promised."

(HEBREWS 11:11)

STORY

When the alarm went off, Ja'nay could not muster up the strength to get out of bed. She did not want to face the same day, the same issues, nor the same job!

"Lord, I can't imagine a change will ever come for me," she said aloud. "I've been waiting for so long that I have become one with my pain and disappointment."

She dragged herself out of bed and opened her daily devotional. The theme for the day was "Sarah, a Lady in Waiting."

As Ja'nay began to read, the message spoke directly to her pain and disappointment. She literally felt like Sarah, a woman waiting on a blessing from God. The devotional indicated that God's timing is His own. He does not follow the schedule of His people. He creates the master schedule.

"I understand, God," Ja'nay whispered as she closed the book. "I will wait on You."

APPLICATION

The story of Sarah in the Bible serves as an example of God doing things His way. God operates according to His own timing and in His own way. He is extraordinary. Therefore, He does not do things in ways that seem normal to us. He operates according to a divine plan in divine order with divine timing.

God does not need our help. Our job is to trust in the possibility even when we cannot see it happening. God is the God of possibilities. All things are possible for those who believe. Every promise that God has made will come to pass. The timing may not be what you want, but it will be perfect timing to accomplish God's intentions.

PRAYER

Father God, I praise You for allowing me to see this day. I am thankful that You are faithful. I praise You because You are always making a way for me. I praise You because You are a miracle worker. I praise You because You are a promise keeper. I trust You, Lord. You have perfect timing concerning my life. In Jesus' name, I pray, Amen.

DAY 3
SALVATION INCREASE

Do you share the story of salvation?

"And when she was baptized, and her household, she besought us, saying, If ye have judged me to be faithful to the Lord, come into my house, and abide there. And she constrained us."

(ACTS 16:15)

STORY

Mrs. Brown was a woman of grit and grace, a woman of determination and brilliance. She launched her own advertising company in her early thirties. Twenty years later, the company was still thriving and she had seven employees, including Ja'nay.

After receiving a clear diagnosis, Ja'nay's faith in God increased and she viewed everything in her life differently. It was as if her eyes were open for the first time to all the positive aspects of the company where she worked. She was excited about the personal care given to larger corporate clients and the details provided to the small business clients that relied on them to assist with their growth. The company even participated in volunteer and community outreach programs!

One day, Ja'nay noticed that something was different about Mrs. Brown. She seemed more withdrawn, almost melancholy. She was not the confident, in-charge woman Ja'nay respected and admired. Ja'nay felt she should do something, but she didn't know what to do.

"God," Ja'nay began, "use me to help Mrs. Brown through whatever is going on in her life right now."

When she opened her eyes, a new email from her church was in her inbox. It was an invitation to a special "Women in Business" service sponsored by the Women's Ministry. Ja'nay decided to invite Mrs. Brown to attend.

"Come in," Mrs. Brown said in response to the knock at her door.

"Hi," Ja'nay said. "I stopped by to invite you to a 'Women in Business' service on Sunday at my church. The program will include a special sermon as well as a networking session afterward. I thought you might enjoy attending."

"That's sounds like an excellent event, Ja'nay," Mrs. Brown replied. "Thank you for inviting me. Please send me all of the details. I look forward to attending."

As Ja'nay turned to leave the office, she couldn't contain her joy.

On Sunday morning, Ja'nay was up and ready for service early! When she entered the sanctuary, she was surprised to see Mrs. Brown already there. She greeted her and sat next to her. At the end of the stirring message, the doors of the church were opened for membership. Mrs. Brown was the first one down the aisle. Ja'nay was overjoyed that Mrs. Brown had found the missing link for increase in her life—salvation.

APPLICATION

Being successful personally and professionally does not always guarantee being successful spiritually. It does not matter how many clothes and shoes you have, how many cars you have, nor how many square feet are in your house if you do not have a relationship with God. Spiritual success can only be attained through a relationship with God. No matter what is going well in your life, if God is not a part of it, it will not last long.

When you reach the level of success you desire, you must continue to seek to grow and expand. Grow even deeper in Christ. Expand your knowledge of the Bible. Reach out to others who may be suffering. God is the secret to success. Do not keep Him secret. Share the love and the Word of God with everyone you meet. Let your life be a living example and a beacon that shines the light of His grace and mercy.

PRAYER

Father God, I thank You for the opportunity to glorify Your Name! Father, it is Your desire to save all humankind, so help me to be a willing and able vessel that tells others about Your goodness and Your grace. Allow my life to be a living example of Your unconditional love. Give me the words to speak as I share Your saving power with others. I want to be a vessel and beacon that leads the lost to You so that they may be saved. In Jesus' name, I pray, Amen.

DAY 4
COURAGE INCREASE

Do you have the courage to speak up?

"For if thou altogether holdest thy peace at this time, then shall there enlargement and deliverance arise to the Jews from another place; but thou and thy father's house shall be destroyed: and who knoweth whether thou art come to the kingdom for such a time as this?"
(ESTHER 4:14)

STORY

LaTosha and Ja'nay had not seen each other for a few weeks, and both were excited about their lunch. When Ja'nay arrived at the restaurant, LaTosha was already seated.

"Hey Girl," Ja'nay beamed as the friends hugged. She could tell something was wrong. "LaTosha, what's going on?" she asked.

As the waiter placed their salads in front of them, LaTosha began telling her friend an incredible story.

One of LaTosha's mentees worked part-time at her job. She was a sweet young girl and a hard worker. The company planned to offer her a more permanent position. When they did a routine background check, it was discovered that the girl was caught shoplifting a few years ago. LaTosha's supervisor told her about the blemish on the record and their plans to let the girl go.

"This will ruin this young girls' self-esteem and it could also cause her to leave the mentoring program," LaTosha said frantically. "The program has changed her life."

"Then talk to your supervisor," Ja'nay recommended.

"I want to do that, but I'm afraid. When I was fifteen, I was caught shoplifting, but I was not charged. Now I am working for this amazing company, in line for another promotion, well-respected, and well-liked. To ask for grace for this young woman could cost me my job, if I am honest about my past. What should I do?"

Ja'nay did not give her friend a direct answer. Instead, she told her the story of Esther in the Bible. Esther wanted to save her people. To do so, she risked everything, including her life. She was courageous enough to ask the king for mercy. Because of the favor of God upon her life, it was granted.

"I know what I have to do," said LaTosha.

When LaTosha returned to work, she told the supervisor her story and asked for a second chance for her mentee. To her amazement, the company agreed to give the young lady a permanent position.

LaTosha couldn't wait to call Ja'nay. She had received and demonstrated an increase in courage, just like Esther.

APPLICATION

Do you have the courage to speak up? When you see something that should be addressed, do you say something or keep going? Can people count on you to defend what is right? It takes courage to step out of the box and to go against the grain. If you do not feel comfortable doing this, then you need an increase in courage.

An increase in courage requires at least two things. First, it requires purpose. In order to increase in courage, you must recognize that you have a purpose. You must understand that you have been placed where you are for a reason. Esther realized she was not placed in the palace just to live a good life for herself. She was placed there to be of service to others. God used her to fulfill His plan for His people. Wherever we are, we must look around for opportunities to be used by God. Each time God uses you, your courage increases.

An increase in courage also requires faith in God. You have to believe that God has equipped you for whatever assignment He has given you. When you know that God has your back, you will not be afraid of the enemy. You will stand up, speak up and even step out in faith armed with courage and covered by God.

PRAYER

Father God, I trust You to direct my life. Father, I know You have a plan for my life. Father, I know there is purpose in my life. Father, give me the insight to see it and the courage to act on it, and I will give You all the glory and all the praise. God, continually be my rock and shield. In Jesus' name, I pray, Amen.

DAY 5
REMEMBRANCE INCREASE

Do you remember your increase?

"Then ye shall answer them, That the waters of Jordan were cut off before the ark of the covenant of the LORD; when it passed over Jordan, the waters of Jordan were cut off: and these stones shall be for a memorial unto the children of Israel for ever."

(JOSHUA 4:7)

STORY

Washing her face, Ja'nay stared at herself in the mirror. She couldn't understand the way she was feeling. She was heavy in spirit and she had not prayed in a few days. Work was feeling like work and she was late for church every Sunday, if she made it at all! Just last month she was in a much better place. Her spirit had been renewed and refreshed. She had experienced increase in several areas of her life, but now it seemed as though she had forgotten all about that.

Ja'nay had been so sure that she was free from all of the doubt, fear, and disappointment that had plagued her most of her adult life. She often felt like she was taking two steps forward and then three steps backward. She called her friend and shared how she felt.

"Just a few short weeks ago, I had amazing encounters with God," Ja'nay explained. "Now, I wonder if any of it was real. My spiritual life has taken a great dive."

"Girl, you just need a good dose of remembrance," her friend Mellody teased. "Do you remember how God healed your body? Do you remember how God mended your broken heart? Do you remember how God answered your prayers for peace? Do you remember the many blessings that He gave you—despite your missteps?"

"I do," said Ja'nay. She was feeling a little embarrassed for even complaining. "Well," Mellody continued, "God has not changed. He is the same God. He is able to do abundantly above whatever you ask or think. Girl, you need to get it together."

"You're right," said Ja'nay. "I have no reason to feel this way. God has been good to me. All of my needs are met and some of my wants."

"Increase," said Mellody. "God has given you increase. Take some time to write down where you were and where you are now because of God's increase. Post the list where you can see it. Every morning when you read that list, you will be reminded you are the Ja'nay of increase not the Ja'nay of doubt! Amen."

Ja'nay followed her friend's advice, and her spirits were immediately lifted each time she remembered just how much God had done for her. She was truly grateful for increase.

APPLICATION

Sometimes we go through periods of depression. We can't put our finger on it, but we know that something is just not right. We don't feel like going to work. We don't want to be around friends and family. We wonder if all of our efforts are worth it. In these times, we seem to forget who we are and whose we are.

My dear sister, when you are feeling down, you have to take time to remember. Remember that you are a child of God. Remember that God has brought you through many situations. Look around you at the blessings, big and small that He has bestowed on you. Document the increase God has given you in every area of your life. Write down your answered prayers, and also thank God daily for His increase.

PRAYER

Father, I love and adore You. You are the only true and living God. Thank You for providing breakthroughs in my life. Thank You for answered prayers. Help me to remember the things that You have done for me. You have delivered me from sin and protected me from danger. You have provided for me and comforted me. Lord, You have brought me from a mighty, mighty long way. Thank You, God, for Your increase. In Jesus' name, I pray, Amen.

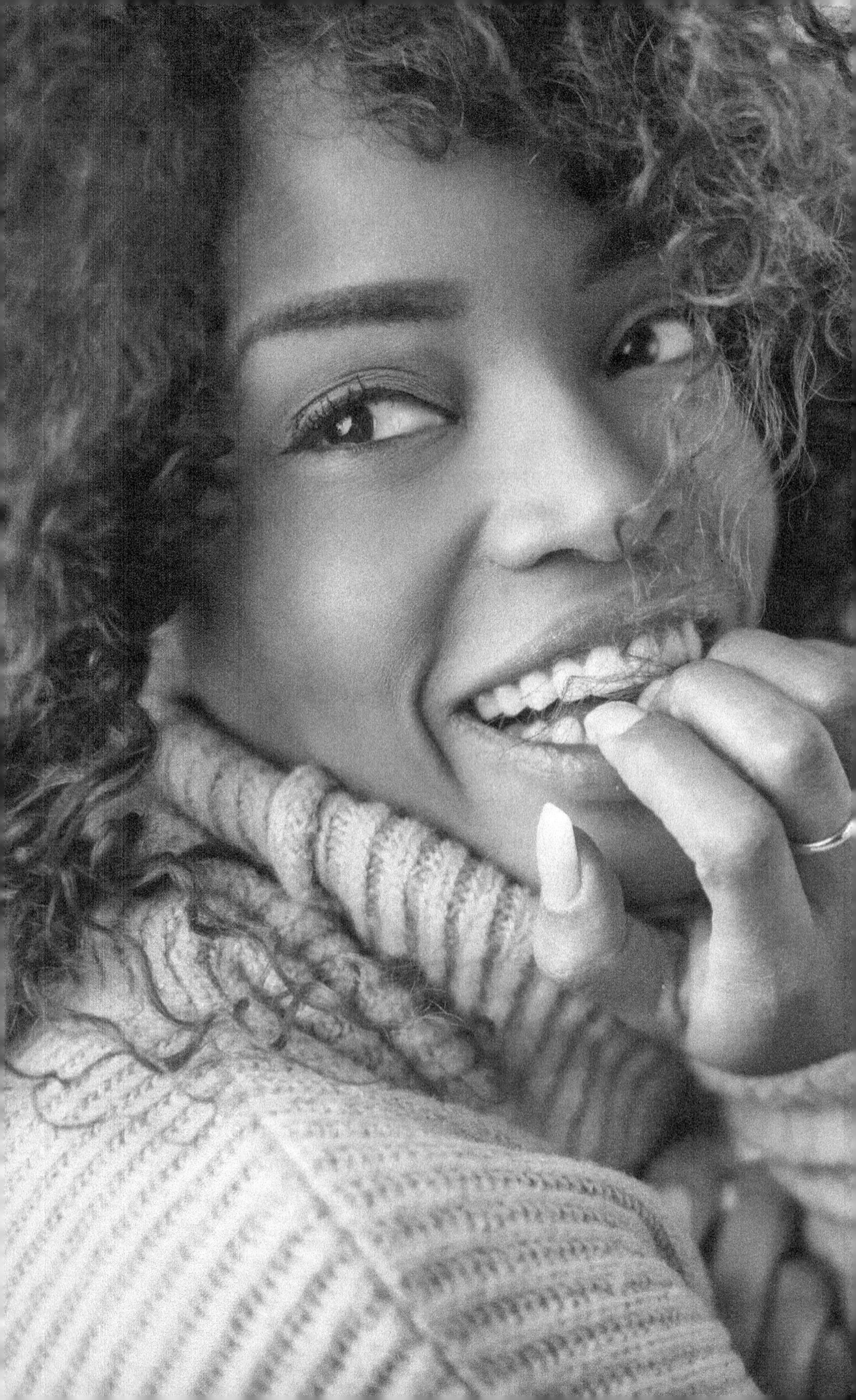

LEARN – DR. LAQUANDA CARPENTER

DAY 1
LEARN THROUGH LESSONS

What lessons have you learned that profoundly affected your life?

"Shew me thy ways, O Lᴏʀᴅ, teach me your paths."
(PSALM 25:4)

STORY

One morning, a booming sound in Ava's garage suddenly awakened her. She got out of bed to see what was happening. As she opened the garage door, she saw her brother, Eli, stumbling to the door. Eli often stayed with her when he and his wife were at odds. On this particular morning, she was not expecting Eli. She had just spoken to her sister-in-law Rain a few days before and things seemed to be going well for them at the time. As Ava looked at Eli, she could tell that he was in a drunken state as he stumbled to her door in an attempt to come inside.

"Eli, what is wrong? Where have you been?" Ava asked with obvious annoyance.

"Rain and I had an argument yesterday evening, and I slept in the car. When I woke up, I drove over here," Eli responded.

"Come in and get yourself together. We can talk later," she promised.

As Ava walked back to her room, she prayed for God to bring peace to her brother's home. She prayed for God to restore her brother's marriage. She wanted Rain and Eli to be happy and enjoy each other's company again. She smiled when she thought of the how much she admired their relationship when they were first married.

APPLICATION

There are times in our lives when we forget the importance of nourishing and sustaining our relationships with our family members, friends, partners, children, church families, etc. All relationships have to be watered with love, forgiveness, and friendship. It takes both people who are involved in the relationship to care for and tend to the relationship.

www.urbanspirit.biz

Oftentimes, we take the persons who are most important to us for granted. We assume that the person will always be there. We allow our tongues to spew angry lingo and insulting commentary. We expect that the person will remain in relationship with us. We believe that what we have said will be ignored and that we will be forgiven. This is not always the case.

God always reminds us that He did not design us to go through life alone. Our relationships require us to demonstrate limitless love, unshakable faith, and endless devotion and support for one another. When we forget that God should be at the center and the core of our relationships, we begin to say and do hurtful things to our loved ones. We must remember that we are God's people. Therefore, we should always walk and talk with love, kindness, respect, and support. When we do not properly nourish our relationships, we completely take the other person for granted. We should always want our loved ones to know that we appreciate them.

PRAYER

Dear God, I pray for my relationships. I pray that You restore peace, love, kindness, patience, forgiveness, and love in each one of them. Lord, I know You are a healer, a restorer, and a teacher. Please teach me how to nurture my relationships with my loved ones and friends. Lord, I do not want to take anyone in my life for granted. Thank You for showing me how to be a great partner, spouse, friend, and colleague. I want everyone in my life to see You through me. In Jesus' name, I pray, Amen.

DAY 2
LEARN THROUGH ANGER

Have you ever been so angry that you hurt the people you say you love?

"But thou, O Lord, art a God full of compassion, and gracious, long suffering, and plenteous in mercy and truth."
(PSALM 86:15)

STORY

On a quiet, sunny morning, Rain decided to get up early enough to enjoy the sunrise, sip a cup of hot tea, and write in her journal. As she reflected, she realized that since the family had been spending more time together, her husband had become

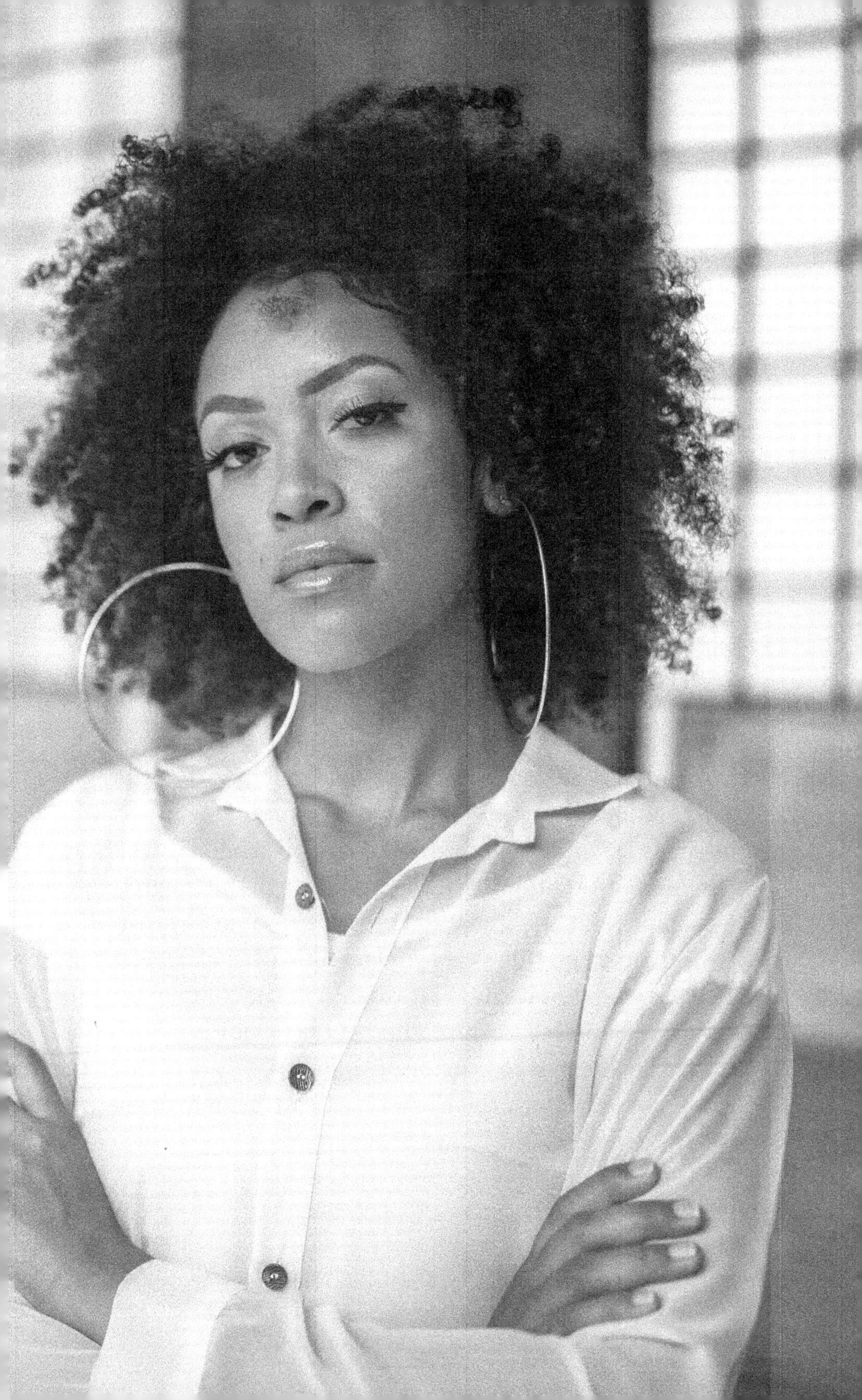

quite impatient with her and the kids. She noticed that Elijah would snap quickly and get angry about small things. If he could not find something, such as his keys or his laptop, he would yell everyone's name. It did not matter what everyone else in the house was doing, he would demand that they stop what they were doing to help him find whatever he had lost. Oftentimes, the missing items were in plain sight.

As the kids grew older, they expressed themselves more. They mentioned their father's behavior to Rain, and she began to notice them clinging to her more than usual. She decided to talk to Elijah about his actions, which she was not fond of at all. Later during the day when she believed Elijah was in a good mood, she approached him to talk. He quickly dismissed her with a very rude response.

APPLICATION

God teaches us to love our friends and family and to treat them with kindness despite what is going on around us. There will be times when life will throw us a curveball and we will have unexpected situations to navigate. Through the tough times, we should treat our family and friends the same way we would treat them when things are going well. We have to learn how to trust God despite difficult times. We should take time to self-reflect and self-correct when our behavior is not what it should be. We must learn how to appropriately deal with our emotions and not use them as an excuse to mistreat the people we say we love.

We should remember that our lives are precious and short. When our loved ones come to us in love with concerns about our behavior, we should listen, reflect, and attempt to change our course. Our goal should be to live as the best versions of ourselves for the persons that we say we love. We should work hard not to give our spouses and close family scraps while giving our co-workers, friends, and church members our best.

Prayer

Lord, I know that I am not my best right now, but I want to be. I know that I need Your help. Please give me the tools, the strength, and the focus to reset myself. You have taught me that I am Your child. Although I make mistakes, it is my responsibility to see the error of my ways and to correct myself through Your guidance. Help me to be what You desire and to walk according to Your will for my life. In Jesus' name, I pray, Amen.

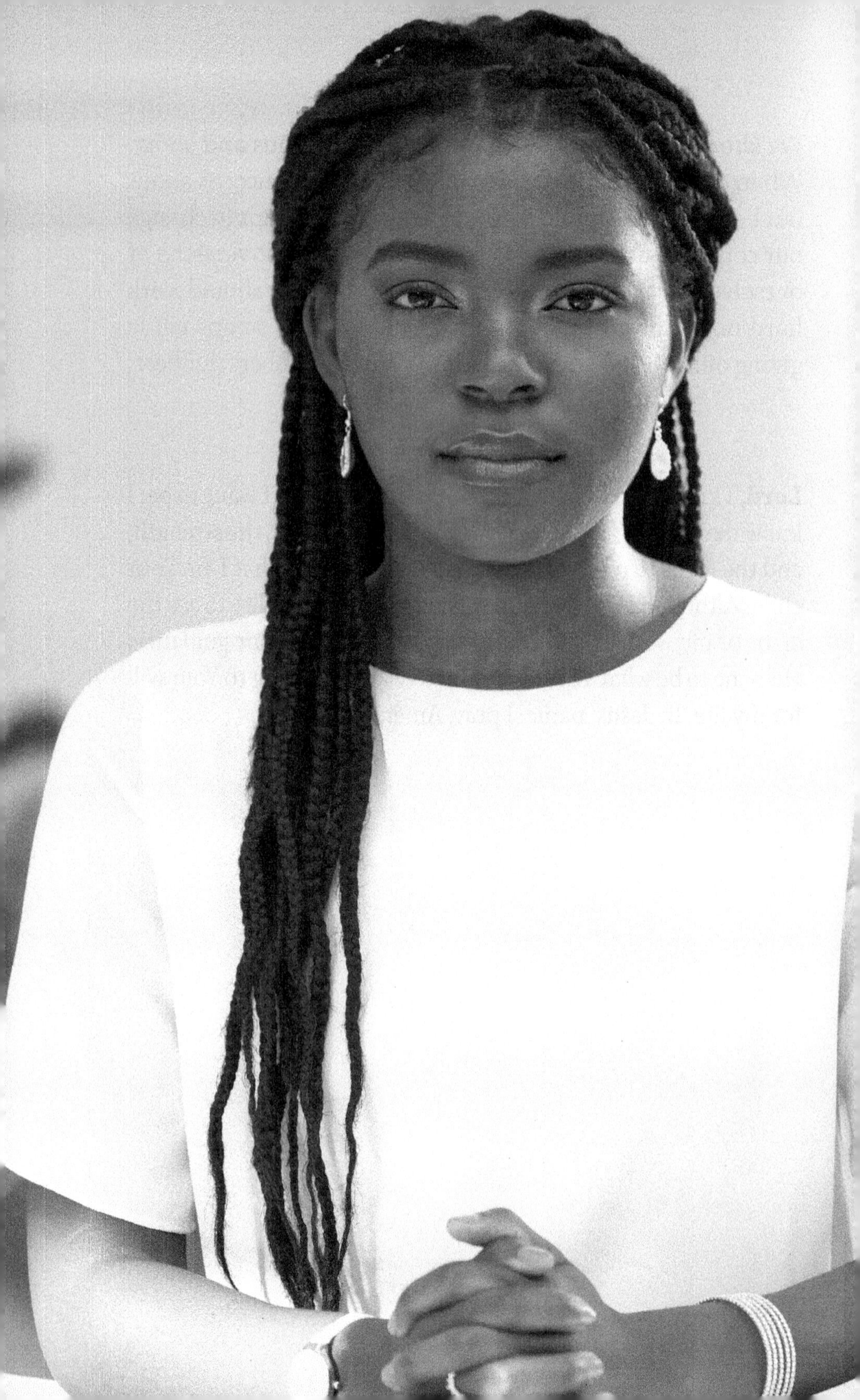

DAY 3
LEARN THROUGH RESTRAINT

How have you used restraint in your decision-making as it relates to your relationships?

"Then Jesus said unto to him, Put up again thy sword into his place: for all they that take the sword shall perish with the sword."
(MATTHEW 26:52)

STORY

Rain found herself having to wait until the right time to approach her husband to discuss her opinion of issues, ask any questions that she may have, or sometimes to simply talk. He was often short, moody, and rude. She reflected on a few recent interactions that she had with him where she walked away from the conversation feeling disrespected and ignored. During one conversation, she remembered him yelling, "Leave me alone!"

Often, Rain would point out to her husband that he talked to everyone else with love, candor, and excitement, but was rude, insulting, and demeaning when speaking to her. Whereas he communicated with his family and friends with a normal tone, he often yelled and screamed at Rain. If he did not approve of a decision that she made, he would respond to the decision with insults, anger, and name-calling.

Rain realized that she felt defeated in her marriage. She did not feel appreciated and was often humiliated. Although most of the disrespectful behavior occurred at home, she reflected on a few moments when her husband had insulted her or taken verbal jabs at her publicly. Rain knew that something had to change.

APPLICATION

God has taught us that love is patient and kind, not arrogant, rude, or mean. Therefore, we should treat our spouses the same way we want our children's spouses to treat them and how we want our parents treated in their relationships. Marriage is one of the most sacred relationships that we can enter. When we share vows with another person, we make a public promise to our spouse, our family, and their family that we will treat each other with kindness, love, respect, gratitude, and adoration. Mistreating our spouses is surely frowned upon by God. When we mistreat our spouse, we are damaging the most sacred relationship that we will ever have here on earth.

Prayer

Lord, forgive me for my sins. Please, Lord, control my tongue and the tongue of my spouse. Guide me to behave, act, and speak in a manner that makes You proud. Help us both not to practice revenge, but to listen and speak with love. I pray Lord that You will speak to my spouse and guide his tongue and his behavior so that our marriage will be one that You are proud of when You look down at us. Help me to be mindful of my words and tone when speaking to my husband. Lord, stand in the midst of our marriage and teach us to love one another and grow together. I pray that our bond is reflective of Your love for the church. In Jesus' name, I pray, Amen.

DAY 4
LEARN THROUGH REGRET

Are you making choices that meet God's approval?

"There is a time for everything, and a season for every activity under the heavens."
(ECCLESIASTES 3:1, NIV)

STORY

As the mornings turned into afternoons, the afternoons turned into evenings and the evenings turn into nights, Rain realized that she was living through her marriage day by day. Some days were good and some days were awful. During the past few months, there had been nothing in middle, just extremes.

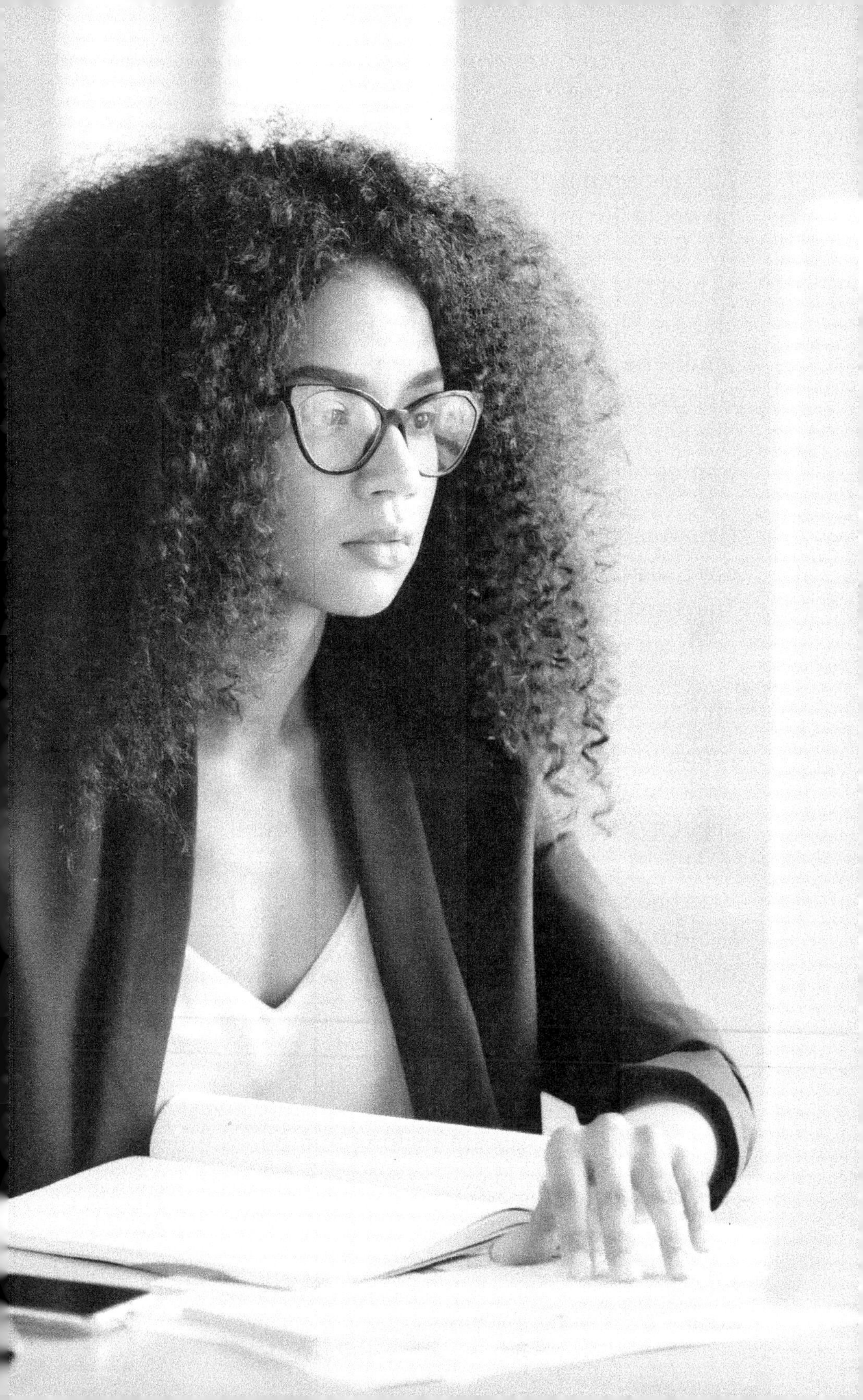

Rain realized that she did not have a voice in her marriage. Eli had begun to make decisions without her, whereas before he would involve her in all decisions. Slowly and surely, Rain was beginning to realize that she did not even feel connected to him anymore. Her husband's behavior and language had shifted. She noticed that when he talked to his friends and family, he would refer to their possessions as "his." He had stopped including Rain in his conversations and interactions. She felt dismissed by her husband and began to wonder if Eli wanted her around anymore.

"I'm so confused," Rain told her friend Lisa. "I never know from day to day what kind of mood Eli will be in when he wakes up. The worst part of it is that he won't talk about what is going on in our marriage."

"That's unfortunate," said Lisa. "I know this sound cliché, but communication is key. There is no way for the two of you to work this out if he won't talk about it. If he won't talk to you about it, then you have to talk to God about it."

Rain had already prayed about her marriage, but she had not heard from God. She knew that she needed to be patient. She couldn't change Eli, but she could work on herself.

Application

Oftentimes, we experience shifts in our lives, we begin to question our decision-making and our ability to judge character. We may even go through a phase of blame and shame. There are times when we may blame ourselves for the state of our relationships when they are not going well. During the process of blame, we will often shame ourselves for not speaking up about a matter sooner, or not being more aggressive. If we have personalities that are calm and quiet, we may even wish or hope for different personality traits. When we play the blame and shame game, God is not pleased or proud of us. He wants us to love who we are just as we are and appreciate Him for designing us according to His divine purpose.

We cannot go through life regretting any of our relationships. Every relationship has a purpose and a season. We have to look to God for guidance and allow Him to lead us where He wants us to go. Even during difficult times, God wants us to pause, reflect, and listen to Him. When we are experiencing difficulties in our relationships, God wants us to pray and talk to Him. We have to believe that God wants us to be happy. During difficult moments, God wants us to do the work in the relationship so that we are giving our partners our absolute best. However, we have to know that we cannot control others, only ourselves.

Prayer

Dear God, I pray for my sister and her husband. I pray that they are able to weather the storm and overcome the challenges that they experience. Help them, Lord, to be the very best version of themselves as individuals and as a collective unit. Thank You for covering their relationship with Your love, protection, and mercy. In Jesus' name, I pray, Amen.

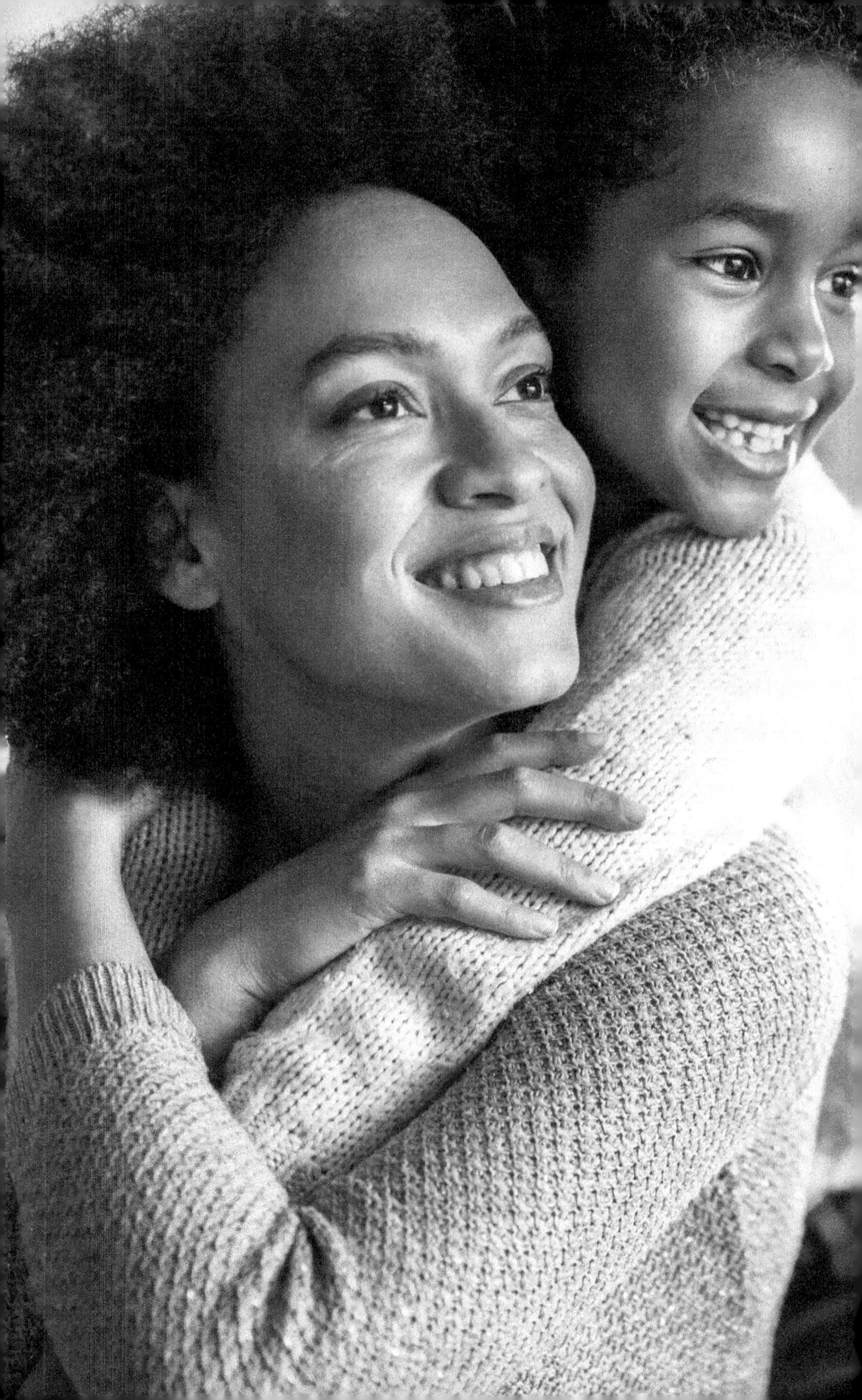

DAY 5
LEARN THROUGH LOVE

How are you learning through love?

"But continue thou in the things which thou hast learned and hast been assured of, knowing of whom thou hast learned them."

(II TIMOTHY 3:14)

STORY

Rain asked God to lead her and guide her because she knew she was in a bad place personally and in her marriage. Instead of focusing on Eli, her husband, Rain decided to focus on herself. She decided to do the work required to improve her mental and spiritual health by seeking help from a spiritual advisor. She began to meet with her spiritual advisor once a week to talk through her feelings and her emotions. Rain was able to openly and honestly share her experiences.

"I feel as if I have lost my voice," she explained. "I find it difficult to speak to Eli because I am unsure of the type of response I might receive. I don't like being talked to negatively, so I would rather just not say anything. I never thought that I would feel uncomfortable talking to my own husband."

"What do you feel when you hold in what you want to say to him," the advisor asked.

"I feel like a child who is afraid of saying the wrong thing and getting in trouble," Rain responded. "I feel restricted, a feeling that I don't like at all."

"Since Eli won't attend any sessions, maybe you can work on communicating with him at home. Try statements like, "When you say or do this, I think or feel this. You can fill in those blanks according to how you feel in that moment. This exercise will help you gain your voice back."

Rain took the advisors advice. The first few times she used the strategy, Eli just stared at her. She didn't give up though because expressing herself made her feel heard. Eventually, he began to respond and their communication increased.

APPLICATION

Women of color are often taught and told, "suck it up," "don't cry," or "just get through it." Of course, we do all of those things, but we also have to realize that we should release our emotions, and that it is okay to cry. When we realize that we are in situations that seem too big for us, we should remember that no situation is too big for God. There will be some troubling times as we maneuver our way through adulthood, but we should always seek God. God wants us to spend time with Him, praying to Him, talking to Him, and seeking His guidance. He is always guiding us, leading the way, and ordering our steps through life.

Sis, it is okay to seek guidance from a spiritual advisor or a therapist. Historically, society has placed shame on seeking help from someone that is a stranger to us, but we must realize that looking to a therapist to talk through situations and to receive guidance is perfectly okay. Talking to our family and friends is helpful at times, but gaining a new perspective is acceptable and important.

Take time to write a list of what is troubling you. Write a prayer for each situation, and watch God do His work. You will be amazed at what your life will look like once you are on the other side of the situation. Study God's Word, seek His guidance and watch Him work.

PRAYER

Dear Lord, I pray for my sister and ask for Your layer of protection and covering over her and her life. Lord, please help my sister to get through this troubling time and help her to be so much better once this storm is over. Lord, I know You are in control and You never put more on Your people than what they can bear. I understand that You have her wrapped in Your arms. Thank You, Lord, in advance for restoring her soul, her spirit, and her life. In Jesus' name, I pray, Amen.

LEAD – KAREN LASCARIS

FEBRUARY
WEEK 13

DAY 1
LEAD WITH PURPOSE

Do you know why you are here?

"And we know that all things work together for good to them that love God, to them who are the called according to his purpose."
(ROMANS 8:28)

STORY

Four times per year, Lisa and her girlfriends paused their busy schedules to come together. Each season, they would choose a different task to complete. One autumn, they created a quilt to honor their ancestors; one spring, they published a manuscript that outlined and celebrated the principles of successful parenting.

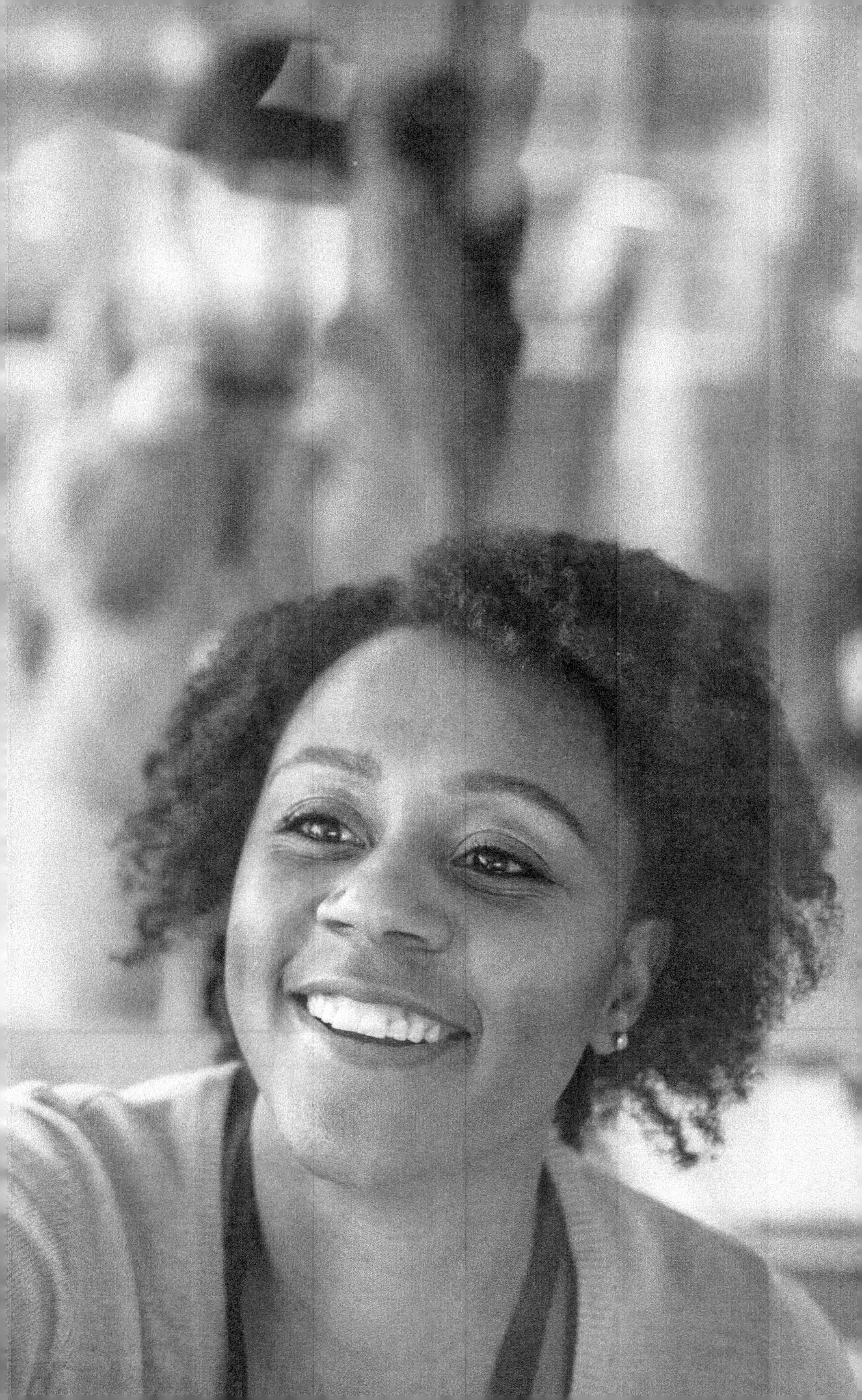

This winter, however, as they each spoke in their virtual meeting room, some women expressed their fears; others wanted to discuss the latest headlines. Karen was in a deeply reflective mood and was last to speak.

"Ladies," she began, "last season, God revealed great leadership from within us. Yet, in this season, we find ourselves fractured by various distractions, even divided by politics. Nevertheless, I believe that God called us together for such a time as this. Before we commit to our next project, let's pray and ask God to carefully search our hearts. Let Him lead us to His will for our work, according to His purpose, not according to what is happening in the world."

At that moment, Lisa felt exposed; she knew she was in a rut. She worked. She consumed media. She slept and then repeated the cycle. She realized that she had never considered her purpose and had no idea of what it was.

APPLICATION

The devil wants to interfere with our purpose. Find those whom he has attacked the hardest, and you will find ones for whom God has a huge calling and purpose for their lives. In the Bible, Joseph endured the envy and treachery of his brothers, as well as lies and imprisonment. Yet, by using his talents—even from his prison cell—he rose to become one of the most powerful men in the land. Job suffered great loss: children, possessions, wealth, and land. Yet, because of his faithfulness, and despite the disagreement of his friends, God restored him and multiplied his wealth. Even Jesus Himself had to endure great pain, torture, and death, in order to fulfill His purpose.

The most important work you can do is to commit to God's purpose for your life. The secret is this—your God-given talents were not given to make you more popular or for you to hoard and hold on to. God blessed you to help someone else. God implanted within you gifts to use to bless someone else. When you use them in this way, He, in turn, blesses you. Love is the key to His kingdom!

Fast, pray, meditate on God's Word, and write the vision He places in your heart. Ask Him to reveal His purpose for your life. Stay free and clear of the world's distractions. Stay focused on God, and He will give you the desires of His heart and yours.

PRAYER

Dear God, my life in You starts today. As I keep my eyes from seeing the violence and evil around me, I no longer fear the report of the world. Instead, I praise You! Lord, use me; please prepare within me a new heart for You; a cleansed sanctuary for Your Holy Spirit. I want to love You with all my heart, all my soul, all my mind, and with my whole body. Stir up the gifts You've created in me before time began. I am here, now, in this season, for Your glory, and I commit to use my talents for Your praise. Lord, I commit to You today, "Not my will, but Your will" be done, throughout all the earth! In Jesus' name, I pray, Amen!

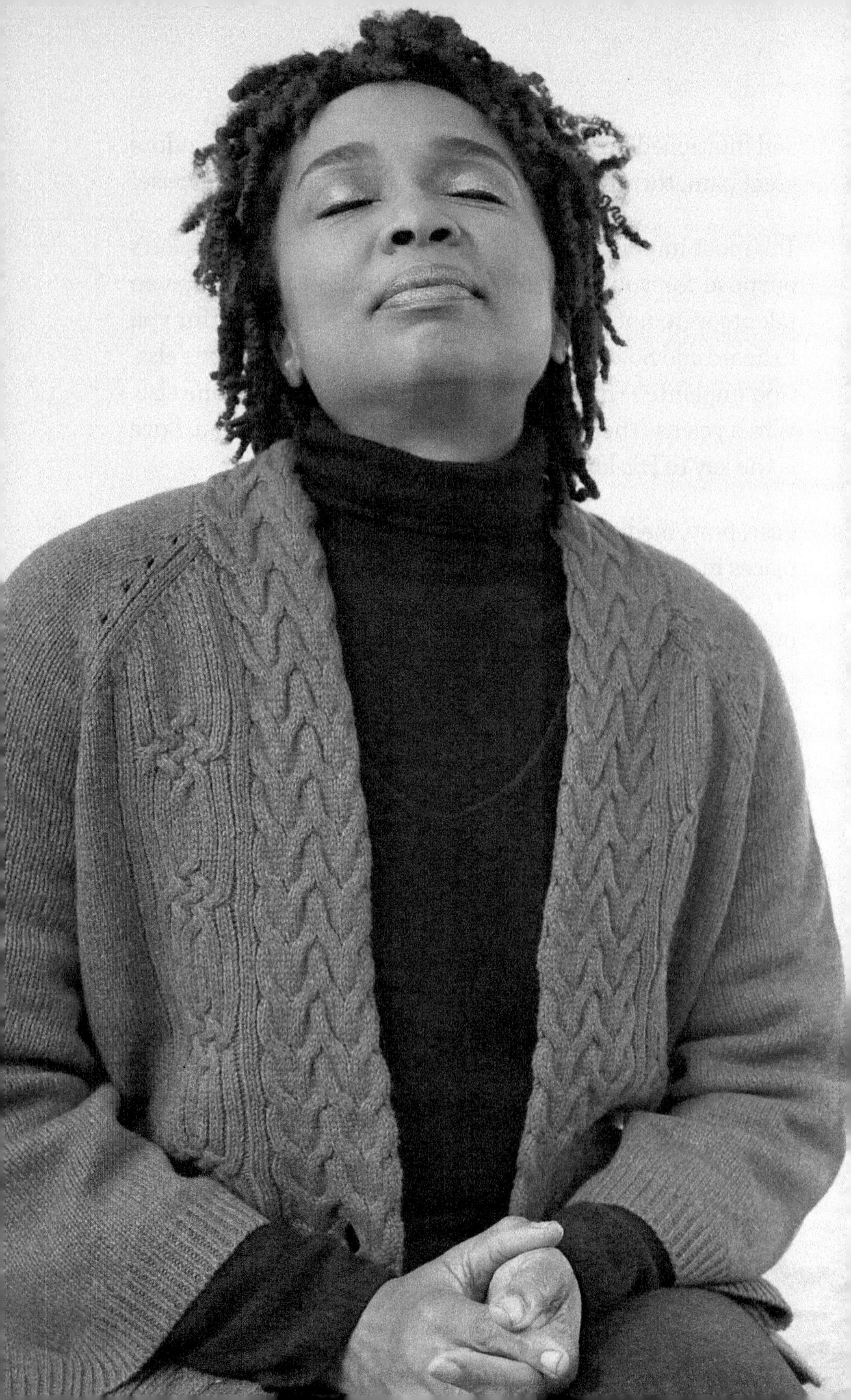

DAY 2
LEAD THROUGH FAITH

Is God calling you to lead…or to follow?

"But the Lord is faithful, who shall stablish you, and keep you from evil."
(II THESSALONIANS 3:3)

STORY

"I don't think I'm cut out for this. Maybe I should quit and do my own thing," Lisa pondered.

Five years ago, when Lisa first interviewed for her current position, she never believed she would have an opportunity to work for such a prestigious firm. She had always imagined that she would start her own business, but when the company created a new position for her, she wondered, *"Could God have a different plan?"*

At first, everyone commended Lisa's work and her future looked promising. As time passed, she watched for years as co-workers moved upward to new opportunities. Lisa was not promoted, and she began to doubt herself.

Finally, there was a glimmer of hope. A powerful female executive with a fresh, new vision joined the company, and Lisa was assigned to work closely with her. For years, their hard work flourished and the company's profits increased. When her boss retired, Lisa was rewarded for five years of stellar work and promoted to department head.

Again, she began to doubt her role at the firm. She had never managed a team before and grumblings in the department exposed hostile co-workers. Without her mentor's protection and leadership, she felt vulnerable, even lost. Her fears began to speak louder than God's voice and she felt unsure of her path.

APPLICATION

When the season shifts in our lives and the path seems unclear, it is important to speak to God in prayer. We must also listen for His answer to discern His voice from our own and to receive His direction. The principle that the Lord expects us to activate, which we often forget, is *faith*.

Examples for us to follow are everywhere throughout the Bible from Joseph, who refused to let go of the dream of greatness God had for his life and eventually ruled a nation, to Esther, who cast out self-doubt to save her people, to Ruth, whose faithful pursuit of wisdom led the world to Jesus.

There is no greater reward in the world than the blessings we receive from God when we have the faith to follow Him. Keep a journal of the triumphs and victories that God has blessed you with along the way; create your own ritual to focus on God at the start of your day. When we fast, pray, and seek His direction, the safety and protection of His wings allow us to leave our fears behind us. When we are not afraid, we walk forward by faith and trust God to lead us. It is faith that empowers us to enter confidently into a new season of change, growth, and blessings, and enables us to see God's promises and miracles manifest in our lives.

PRAYER

Heavenly Father, You are almighty and all-powerful. To You, I give thanks, glory, and praise. I humble myself before You today to ask Your forgiveness for my doubt. Please search me for my hidden faults and cleanse me until I look more like You. Please grant me the wisdom to honor the unique vision You have for my life. Lord, I pray that You send Your Holy Spirit to renew my faith and my strength. Please cover me with Your mighty wings as I follow Your will. I pray that You help me to keep my eyes straight ahead as I walk on the path You have placed before me, a path that leads not to my own desires or to man's rewards, but to the fullness of You. In Jesus' name, I pray, Amen.

www.urbanspirit.biz

DAY 3
LEAD WITH OBEDIENCE

Do you run before your walk?

"For he shall give his angels charge over thee, to keep thee in all thy ways. They shall bear thee up in their hands, lest thou dash thy foot against a stone."

(PSALM 91:11-12)

STORY

After a brief illness, Lisa heard God say, "Go out and start walking." She had not exercised in at least fifteen years, so she had no doubt it was His voice. The next morning, she started a vigorous, thirty-minute health walk as part of her daily ritual.

Five days a week, Lisa walked at sunrise. Her mind was clearer and her lungs felt stronger.

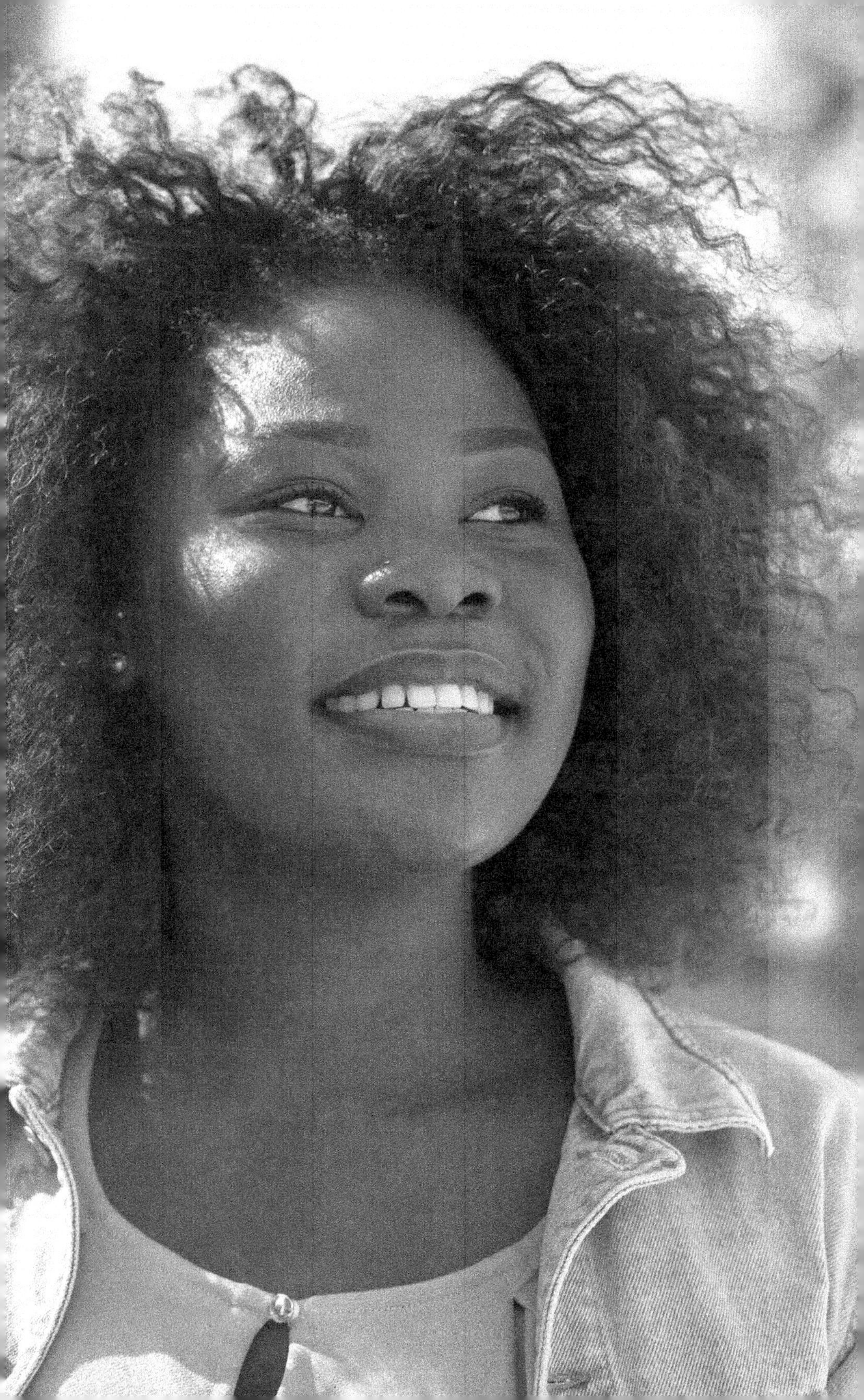

She thought she would step it up by adding a little jogging to her routine too. She was a good runner in high school, and she was quite a bit thinner back then. *"Maybe,"* Lisa thought, *"jogging can make my body leaner now too."*

After Lisa increased her pace, she felt great! She jogged two miles in no time and she could not believe she had gotten back into her old stride. Just then, Lisa hit a crack in the pavement and fell, hands first.

Before she even had a chance to assess the damage, two women appeared at either side of her. Two charge nurses from the nearby hospital immediately reached down to offer Lisa an arm of support. When she rose to her feet, Lisa felt no pain at all, but she learned a very hard lesson that day.

APPLICATION

God has many ways of speaking to us, including through His Word, with His voice, and through Jesus Christ. When He speaks, He gives us instruction. He reveals His expectation for us to lead a life of obedience.

In the Bible, Abraham was tested by God. He was given the unthinkable command to kill his beloved son as a sacrifice. Abraham obeyed, and in the midst of preparing the sacrifice, God sent an angel to spare the son and provide a different sacrifice. Because he obeyed God's voice, Abraham was rewarded with abundance. God promised to bless him and to multiply his descendants.

Our small desires are no match for the infinite miracles and blessings we gain through obedience to God. When you pray and meditate on the Word each day, remember the times when you strayed from following God's will for your life and write them in a journal. Then, write the ways in which you returned to Him by being obedient to His will and to His ways. Write how God rewarded you for your obedience and how He blessed you. When you read His Word, listen for His voice and run with obedience to do whatever He commands. God rewards us with an unending flow of blessings. It is obedience to that protects us, even when we stumble in life.

PRAYER

Almighty Father, to You be the glory! I am humbled by Your majesty and might. I thank You for Your grace, mercy, and power. Lord, I ask You today for the strength to trust You, and to obey You. Please search my heart that You might reveal any motives that are not of You. To those who obey Your commands, Your promises are "Yes" and "Amen," and to You I devote my walk. Please send Your angels to cover me with their wings. You have promised in Your Word that they will have charge over me; that, with their hands, they will help me stay balanced, protect me when I slip, and keep me from falling away from You. Please let my life be a testament to Your greatness, and to lead others to the love You show to those whose obedience is to You. In Jesus' name, I pray, Amen.

DAY 4
LEAD WITH DISCERNMENT

Do you hear what God hears and say what He says?

"Death and life are in the power of the tongue: and they that love it shall eat the fruit thereof."
(PROVERBS 18:21)

STORY

"Dear Lord, please give me words to say," Lisa prayed. "Bless me with Your answers and with Your wisdom."

Lisa's mother, Mrs. Gentry, seemed confused lately. She was unable to navigate the activities she loved. Lisa and her older brother Jake rarely agreed, and understanding their mother's condition was no exception.

Jake, a doctor, had examined their mother. He consulted a colleague about his findings and the two agreed to the diagnosis of a fatal disease. They prescribed medications that she should take for the rest of her life. The medication would not cure the disease, but help her to manage it. According to Lisa's research, doctors could not actually diagnose this disease until after death. Therefore, she refused to accept the diagnosis.

"Jake," Lisa said passionately, "think clearly. God is not the author of confusion!"

"What's that supposed to mean?" her brother asked.

"It means that if Mom is confused, then God is not present. This disease kills: it steals and destroys. Mom's belief in Jesus means *life*. So if we haven't found something to save her life, then have we really researched enough?"

Still, Jake sadly accepted the medical research and statistics. When Lisa prayed, meditated, and sought more information, God showed her evidence that their Mom suffered not from a fatal illness, but from taking too many prescription medications.

APPLICATION

The experts in our world today want us to believe that science holds the final answer. Facts in the physical realm are at the end of their story. However, our obedience to a life in Jesus Christ reveals infinite blessings, wisdom, and miracles when we believe in Him.

Lead with Discernment

God gives His people the power of discernment, to distinguish His truth above all else. While in the wilderness, Satan continually tempted Jesus. Satan took Him high atop the pinnacle of a building, then even higher to a mountaintop to entice Jesus with the worship of riches, kingdoms, and even Satan himself! How foolish would it be for Jesus to worship the limited kingdom of Satan when Jesus Himself already owns it all? He has the infinite power of God!

Jesus wants us to be in agreement with Him, to discern His voice above all others, and to know that we have His power too. Pray to Him daily for the discernment to know His heart. Seek only the wisdom revealed by the complete Word of God. When the Word speaks to you, write what you hear and trust the instructions God gives you. When we turn away from the world and its sinful ways and confess that Jesus is the Savior of the world, God's miracles are ours.

PRAYER

Father God, You sent Jesus Christ to be our Shepherd, a light by day and by night. I am so grateful for the invitation to be part of Your flock and to follow Your instruction. Lord, I know that life in You provides me with Your eyes to see, Your Words to speak, and Your ears to hear Your voice. I ask You to bless me with Your power and I thank You for the supernatural ability of discernment. When I am in agreement with You, You bless my life with wisdom, good health, the safety and protection of angels, and the miracle-working power of Jesus Christ, our Lord and Savior. Therefore, I commit my life to You today. I seek You with my whole heart and desire to walk in Your ways and to give You glory, honor, and praise. In Jesus' name, I pray, Amen.

www.urbanspirit.biz

DAY 5
LEAD WITH REPENTANCE

Do you really know what it means to repent?

"I indeed baptize you with water unto repentance. but he that cometh after me is mightier than I, whose shoes I am not worthy to bear: he shall baptize you with the Holy Ghost, and with fire."

(MATTHEW 3:11)

STORY

Lisa tried to keep her volume low as she voiced the pain she felt when she fell down the steps. She grunted with a tightly closed mouth, hoping not to draw too much attention.

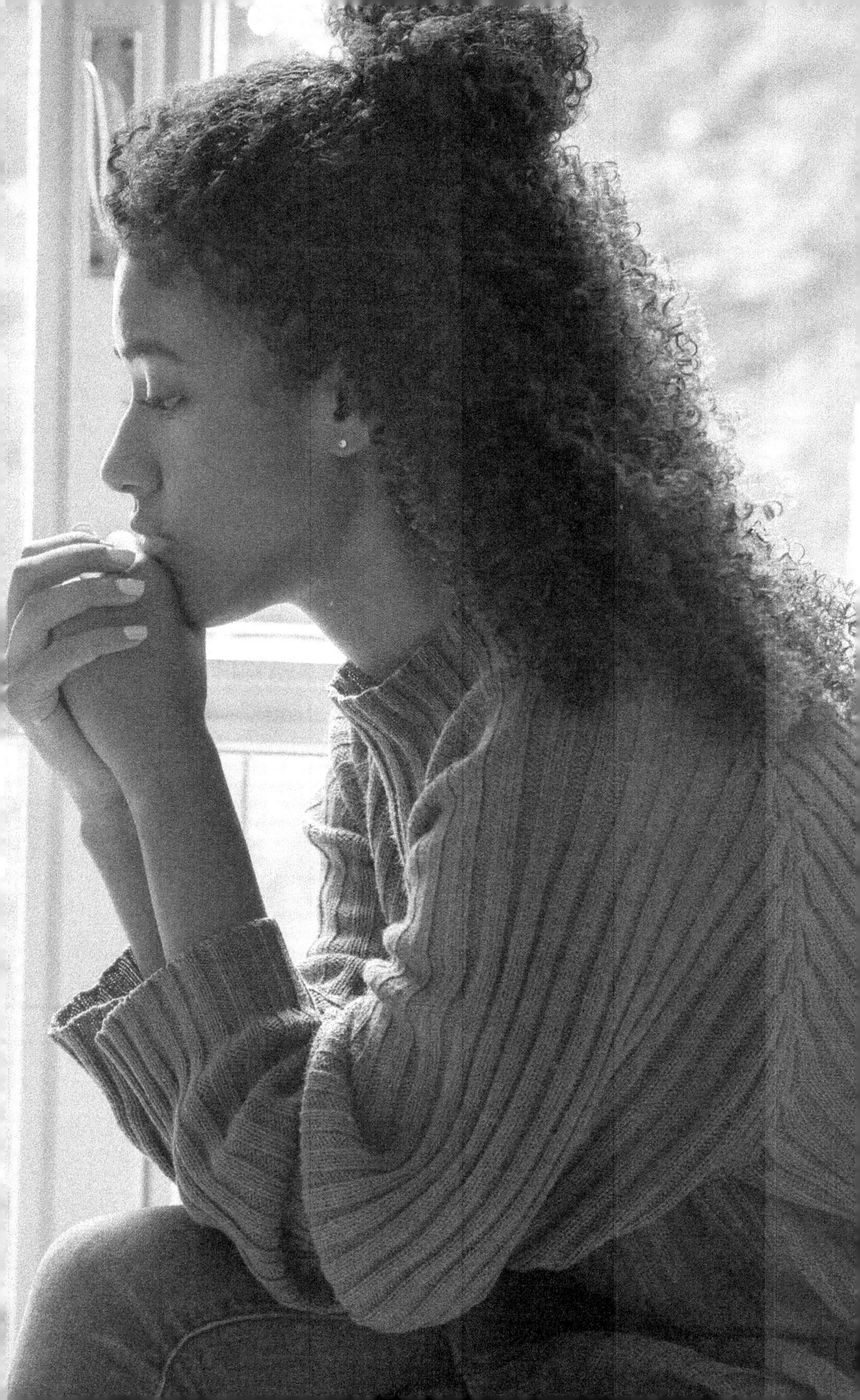

Pastor Williams reached down to help Lisa balance on her good foot. "Take it easy," he said as he reached his hand out to help her up. "You were wearing the wrong shoes today," he chuckled.

The pastor's great sense of humor was not much comfort for Lisa. This was her second fall in a matter of months. This time she fell in a pair of new high-heel shoes as she exited church. She was in so much pain from the sprained ankle that she did not have the energy to feel embarrassed.

Out of work due to her swollen ankle, Lisa had no choice but to sit still. She took the time to meditate on her life. Prayerfully, she asked God to reveal His purpose for her life and she began to walk in it. She stepped out in faith and now she has her own business. She uses her gifts and talents to help others as God directs.

APPLICATION

Trials and tribulations are actually blessings in disguise. We have to take the time to see them through God's eyes. When we allow God to do His perfect work through our repentance, our trials in life actually transform us into fresh new beings, rather than break us down. Our tribulations produce resilience. Resilience produces moral character and character produces hope.

When everything else around us crumbles and the world falls apart, our love of God keeps us strong. His weapons and His benefits give us protection. Through His son, Jesus Christ, He

Lead with Repentance

gives us His Holy Spirit, not the spirit of fear, but of power, love, and the ability to make sound decisions.

You were born to be holy; you are called to a life of holiness. When we fall, God gives us power to get up and to change our ways. Repent, strengthen your weaknesses, and renew a steadfast spirit within yourself. Praise God with your gifts and your whole being; devote your life to Him. Be intentional! Through our love of God, our belief in Jesus Christ and through the power of the Holy Spirit, healing, abundant life, angels, and miracles are indeed possible.

PRAYER

Heavenly Father, today, I bow humbly before You to give You praise, glory, and honor. Thank You for Your goodness. Through Jesus Christ, You have shown me that Your grace, mercy, patience, and love endure forever and ever. You've provided me with so many gifts, miracles, blessings, and benefits that I must make room for them. I am grateful and I thank You. Lord, You provide me with a steadfast spirit to renew my mind; You release Your angels to guide my steps, and You perform Your perfect work in me, which transforms my life. You have shown me that You make all things new. For the blessing of repentance through the power of Your Holy Spirit, and for the opportunity to live the abundant life You have created me for, I thank You. Hallelujah! In Jesus' name, I pray, Amen.

BIOS

Stephanie Perry Moore – General Editor

Stephanie Perry Moore is the trailblazing author of the Payton Skky Series, the first African American, Christian teen series. She has written over seventy-five titles for children and adults. Her newest series is the Magic Strong Series for young readers with Crabtree Publishers. In addition to writing her own titles, she is the General Editor of several Bible products. Some of the releases include *Men of Color Study Bible*, *Wisdom and Grace Bible for Young Women of Color*, and the *Women of Color Devotional Bible*. Other titles that will be released this year are *Strength and Honor Bible for Young Men of Color*, *Women of Color Cookbook*, *Wisdom and Grace Devotional Bible*, and the *African-American Family Bible*. She is the Co-editor of REAL, an urban BibleZine published by Thomas Nelson and the Co-founder of the Sister's in Faith brand. She is the Co-executive Editor for the Breathe Life Bible with HarperCollins Christian Publishing that will release in 2024. She speaks in schools across the nation, uplifting youth. She also works on various film projects. She lives in the greater Atlanta, Georgia area with her husband, Derrick Moore. They have three new adults. Visit her website at www.stephanieperrymoore.com [stephanieperrymoore.com]

Dr. Charrita Danley Quimby – Content Editor

Dr. Charrita Danley Quimby is an author, editor, publisher, and educator. Founder of CDQ Consultants, she provides writing, editing, and publishing services to a broad range of clients. Passionate about creating stories, Charrita is the author of the novel, *Through the Crack*, which chronicles a family's struggle to overcome drug addiction. She has contributed to and/or edited projects, including several editions of the *Women of Color Daily Devotional* and the upcoming *African-American Family Bible*. Currently, Charrita serves as Vice President and Chief of Staff at Hampton University and Director of the Hampton University Press. A member of Delta Sigma Theta Sorority, Inc., she attended Tougaloo College, Louisiana State University, and Georgia State University, earning the BA, MA, and PhD degrees in English, respectively. A native of Mississippi, Charrita is married to Dr. Ronald Quimby, and their family includes one son and two daughters.

Tia McCollors – WEEK 1/WARMTH

Tia McCollors is a bestselling author, speaker, and writing coach. Her first Christian novel, *A Heart of Devotion,* was an Essence Magazine bestseller. Other bestselling titles followed, including *Zora's Cry, The Last Woman Standing,* and *Steppin' Into the Good Life.* Her Days of Grace Series (*Friday Night Love, Sunday Morning Song,* and *Monday Morning Joy*) continues to grow in popularity. In addition to ten novels, Tia has penned several non-fiction projects, including a devotion titled, *If These Shoes Could Talk.* When she is not writing, she finds passion in delivering inspiring and faith-based messages to women about how to maximize their lives. She is a member of Alpha Kappa Alpha Sorority, Inc. Her enthusiastic messages encourage women to embrace their true calling, journey through life with purpose, and cultivate the confidence and dedication to meet their goals. Tia and her husband, Wayne, live with their three children in the greater Atlanta area.

Sherryll Atkins – WEEK 2/COMFORT

Sherryll Atkins is a screenwriter who has written for television and is currently venturing into feature films. Her reading palette includes the Bible, biblical and Hebrew history, as well as young adult fantasy literature. One of her goals is to become a published author in the young adult genre. She lives in Northern California.

Mariah Crews – WEEK 3/HIBERNATE

Rev. Mariah Crews, known as "Rev. Mimi" graduated from Hampton University in 2014. She is blessed to serve as the Minister to teens and college students at Kingdom Fellowship A.M.E. Church. Rev. Mimi was ordained an itinerant Deacon in the A.M.E. Church in 2017. She has always been extremely involved in mentoring and working with the youth. Her goal is to help everyone find their power to walk in confidence and to walk in Christ because only then will they be unstoppable. Rev. Mimi worked in the television industry for a large portion of her career. She began at C-SPAN and was able to work with NBC in Russia during the 2014 Olympic Games. Rev. Mimi is a proud member of Delta Sigma Theta Sorority, Inc. and serves at the organization's headquarters in Washington, D.C. as a specialist helping to promote positive black imagery in the community.

BIOS

Rev. Dr. Robin E. Henderson-Wilson – WEEK 4/DECORATE

Educator. Counselor. Ordained Minister. Mindfulness Trainer. These are just a few of the terms that describe **Robin E. Henderson-Wilson**, PhD's professional accomplishments. As a recognized leader in the fields of counseling and education, Dr. Robin as she is often called, earned her undergraduate degree at Butler University and her subsequent graduate degrees at Indiana University (MA in counseling) and Ball State University (PhD in education). Robin is a dedicated and compassionate leader who dares those around her to take risks. Most recently, she has teamed up with *Mindful Momentum* to develop a program that will empower leaders to use mindfulness to propel their organizations forward. Robin's sincere faith, charismatic personality, and innovative ideas have established her as a highly sought-after preacher, consultant, counselor, and educator. She is a forward-thinking, God-loving individual who consistently challenges herself and those around her to show up as the masterpiece God created every single day.

Rev. Dr. Billie Boyd-Cox – WEEK 5/CELEBRATION

Dr. Billie Boyd-Cox serves as the pastor of Macedonia Baptist Church, Conyers, Georgia. The first woman to serve as pastor of a historic African American Baptist Church in Rockdale County, she currently serves on the Board of Directors for Phoenix Pass and is the recipient of numerous awards and citations. Dr. Cox earned a BS degree, summa cum laude, in organizational leadership from Mercer University, a Master of Divinity degree from McAfee School of Theology, and a Doctor of Ministry degree, summa cum laude, from the Interdenominational Theological Center. She is also a graduate of Leadership Rockdale. She is a realtor, Founder of Open Door Ministries International, CEO of Beyond the Walls Coaching and Consulting, LLC, and the author of three books. Dr. Cox resides in Oxford, Georgia with her family.

Kayla A. Monroe – WEEK 6/WONDER

Kayla A. Monroe, MBA, is a young professional in corporate America who loves pushing the envelope to get people to be comfortable with the uncomfortable. She grew up in a Christian household, but is enjoying her twenties learning, loving, and finding God for herself all while figuring out this thing called, *adulting*. She enjoys anything relaxing from laying out on the beach in new countries to knitting and bingeing new Netflix series! As a member of Alpha Kappa Alpha Sorority, Inc., she enjoys being of service to all mankind. As an aspiring philanthropist, Kayla has her hands in many volunteering efforts ranging from serving on various boards, such as the Springfield Public Forum, to frequently providing workshops to local young women to teach them the importance of personal finance, to her favorite—building houses with Habitat for Humanity around the world! She lives in Connecticut, where she is only thirty minutes from her childhood home and parents.

www.urbanspirit.biz

Evangelist Terri L. Hannett – WEEK 7/FIRE

Terri L. Hannett is the Executive Director of The Church Of God In Christ Publishing House, Crossroads Consulting Group, and the former Vice President of National Accounts for UMI. For over twenty-one years, she has been committed to analyzing the needs of African American Christian organizations and denominations throughout the United States. Evangelist Hannett equips church leaders with training and resources to transform their communities by developing and marketing executable programs. A certified trainer with Darkness to Light Stewards of Children®, ETA (Evangelical Training Association), degree® (Say yes to no debt), and Apna Ghar Domestic Violence, Evangelist Hannett serves on advisory boards for the Hampton University Ministers Conference and Prime Program. Her lifelong goal is to embrace the challenge of addressing the multifaceted needs of the body of Christ.

First Lady Kelli Jones – WEEK 8/LIGHT

Kelli Ann Jones hails from southern Illinois. She came to know the Lord as a child through the loving guidance of an aunt. While pursuing her undergraduate degree in education at Trinity International University, she met her husband, Watson. They currently live in Chicago, IL where Watson serves as a senior pastor and have three beautiful children. Kelli currently works as a special education teacher.

Minister Shantel M. Moore – WEEK 9/GO

Shantel M. Moore has been an active member and leader of New Beginnings Church in Matthews, NC, since February 2000. She is a devoted wife, mother, grandmother, lay counselor, and teacher. She has been a licensed minister since November of 2007, and she has a Bachelor of Science in human resource management from Park College University. She is highly administrative, and she is a veteran of the United States Air Force. As the founder of LC By Design, LLC, she shares her love of drawing, painting, graphic arts, and writing with the world. Shantel's God-given mission is to help people realize their life's purpose. Her goal is to "Bring out the color in your life."

C. Denise Hendricks – WEEK 10/LISTEN

C. Denise Hendricks is an award-winning television producer and writer. She has worked in the news and entertainment industry for CNN, HLN, "The Oprah Winfrey Show," BET's "The Mo'Nique Show," and for ABC, NBC, and CBS television stations across the country. She is currently Executive Producer at MSNBC for the Cross Connection with Tiffany Cross and the Sunday Show with Jonathan Capehart. Denise holds a BS in journalism from Florida A&M University and an MA in Christian education from the Interdenominational Theological Center. She's the recipient of several awards, including an Emmy for Best Newscast, an NAACP Image award, FAMU's Distinguished Alumni Award, and the National Coalition of 100 Black Women's Unsung Heroine Award for her volunteer work with youth. Denise is a member of Delta Sigma Theta Sorority, Inc., the Producers Guild of America, and the National Association of Black Journalists. She is passionate about initiatives surrounding foster care and adoption.

First Lady Jamell Meeks – WEEK 11/LIKE

First Lady Jamell Meeks is the Director of Women's Ministries for the Salem Baptist Church of Chicago, under the leadership of her husband, Reverend James T. Meeks. Women of Influence serves over four thousand women. She serves as National Chair for First Ladies Health Initiative and leader of a national pastors' wives prayer group. First Lady Meeks has been featured in several national publications for her work with entrepreneurship, women, and health. She is a certified John Maxwell speaker and speaks to hundreds of women annually. She developed the nationally recognized A.R.I.S.E Entrepreneur Program in 2004. The program has helped over 1,100 people start and grow their small businesses. Her mission is to inspire women of all ages to live a life grounded by faith, guided by purpose, and motivated by infinite possibilities. She resides in Chicago, Illinois with her husband. She is the mother of four children and a proud grandmother of four.

Dr. Laquanda Carpenter – WEEK 12/LEARN

Dr. LaQuanda Carpenter has served in the education field for more than twenty years in Georgia and Missouri, working in all settings, K–12. Dr. Carpenter is a highly skilled school leader, public speaker, and visionary. She has experience in traditional public schools, public-charter schools, and private schools. Dr. Carpenter has expertise in student and staff empowerment, teacher development and leadership, school transformation and turn-around, inclusion, equity, and databased decision-making. As a school principal, Dr. Carpenter has been an advocate for ensuring that all students within a school building are treated with dignity, respect, love, and care. Furthermore, she often shares educational, historical, and political viewpoints as a youth and women's empowerment speaker. Dr. Carpenter lives in the Kansas City, Missouri area with her husband, Dr. Dennis L. Carpenter, and their two young children.

Karen Lascaris – WEEK 13/LEAD

New Jersey-born **Karen Lascaris** is the author of In Our Own Image: Treasured African American Traditions, Journeys and Icons (Running Press, Philadelphia, 2001). It is the first visual document of African American spiritual, social, and cultural history from WWII to the present. Karen's career began in New York City where she studied communications design at Brooklyn's Pratt Institute. As an illustrator, she has worked with such clients as Revlon, United Airlines, Lincoln Center, and the United Negro College Fund. Through her design talents, she became the first African American Creative Director of the Ralph Lauren Design Studio. Karen's work has taken her around the globe and includes the worlds of art, entertainment, nonprofits, and ministry. She is currently a long-time writer for West Angeles Church of God In Christ in Los Angeles, CA, where she currently resides with her husband, Kellet.

☑ GOALS

Become an US Urban Spirit! Publishing and Media Company Independent or Church Distributor Today!

- earn extra money
- engage with more people
- change lives
- join a winning team
- distribute high-quality Bibles and books

Go to www.urbanspirit.biz

Order your Independent or Church Distributor "Starter Kit" today online. It contains everything you need to get started selling right away.
Or call **800.560.1690** to get started today!

LARGE PRINT

WOMEN of COLOR
DAILY DEVOTIONAL

Fall
EDITION
2

$16.99
ISBN 979-8-9853690-6-9
51699

LARGED PRINT

WOMEN COLOR
DAILY DEVOTIONAL

Spring
EDITION

$14.99
ISBN 978-0-9846480-9-2

WOMEN of COLOR
DAILY DEVOTIONAL

Summer
EDITION

$14.99
ISBN 978-0-9881958-2-0
51499
9 780988 195820

LARGED PRINT

WOMEN of COLOR
DAILY DEVOTIONAL

Fall EDITION

$14.99
ISBN 978-0-9884572-6-3

LARGED PRINT

WOMEN of COLOR
DAILY DEVOTIONAL

Winter
EDITION

$14.99
ISBN 978-0-9884572-2-5